# Sarah Bernhardt
## A French Actress on the English Stage

# Berg Women's Series

## In preparation

*Overleaf*
Sarah Bernhardt as Phèdre, photograph by Nadar, Enthoven Collection

# Sarah Bernhardt

## A French Actress on the English Stage

*Elaine Aston*

**BERG** *Oxford / New York / Munich*

Distributed exclusively in the US and Canada by
St Martin's Press, New York

# For Peter – Always

Published in 1989 by
**Berg Publishers Limited**
Editorial offices:
77 Morrell Avenue, Oxford OX4 1NQ, UK
165 Taber Avenue, Providence, RI 02906, USA
Westermühlstraße 26, 8000 München 5, FRG

**British Library Cataloguing in Publication Data**

Aston, Elaine
 Sarah Bernhardt: a French actress on
 the English stage. — (Berg women's series)
 1. France. Theatre. Acting. Bernhardt,
 Sarah — Biographies
 I. Title
 792′.028′0924

 ISBN 0-85496-019-8

**Library of Congress Cataloging-in-Publication Data**

Aston, Elaine.
 Sarah Bernhardt: a French actress on
 the English stage / Elaine Aston.
 p. cm. — (Berg women's series)
 Bibliography: p.
 Includes index.
 ISBN 0-85496-019-8: $22.00 (est.)
 1. Bernhardt, Sarah, 1844–1923—Appreciation—
 England. 2. Actors—France—Biography. 3. Theater—
 England—London—History.
 I. Title. II. Series.
 PN2638.B5A77 1989
 792′.028′0924-dc19
 [B]                                                     88–36911

Printed in Great Britain by
Billing & Sons Ltd, Worcester

# Contents

# Illustrations

Frontispiece and photos 2, 3 and 5 reproduced by permission of
the Victoria and Albert Museum, London.

# Preface

During research for a doctoral thesis on the work of nineteenth-century English and French actresses, I discovered that one actress loomed constantly over all the others – Sarah Bernhardt. Sarah, the illegitimate daughter of a courtesan, rose from her inauspicious origins to become a major international star of the stage for well over half a century. Her headstrong and independent nature brought her into perpetual conflict with the French critics and her national theatre; but she found a second home in London, and was a favourite with English audiences from her first season in 1879 until her last, two years before her death in 1923. It is the English reaction to the French actress which forms the basis of this study.

As many of the biographies offer conflicting reports and dates, I have relied heavily on newspaper reviews for greater accuracy in determining production dates and critical response. Where recourse to bibliographical documentation has been necessary, I have turned to Ernest Pronier's *Sarah Bernhardt: une vie au théâtre*, which proved the most helpful and accurate source for tabling Paris events and productions.

Some of the information for this study was compiled during my doctoral research; in particular, the chapter entitled 'Male Guises' emerged from a study of the *travesti* genre included in the thesis.

Although there are several biographies of Sarah, the majority were published towards the end of her life or soon afterwards, and it is hoped that this latest study will serve as an introduction to the actress and as a reappraisal of her place in English theatre history, in the light of more recent scholarship.

# 1 Beginnings

'Our family, which is decided for us, scarcely matters, only the people we love count, and above all, the family we create for ourselves.'[1] Thus reflected Sarah Bernhardt at the close of her life. Her statement is a succinct expression of the lifelong antipathy she entertained towards the institutions of marriage and family – far too restricting for a self-willed and independent nature, such as hers. Throughout her life, her erratic career and private behaviour were viewed mostly as objects of prurient fascination which, on occasion, would spill over into outright moral indignation, none of which, however, ever induced Bernhardt to conform.

Disdaining the conventional values of her time, Bernhardt did nothing to dispel the speculations and rumours surrounding her origins. She offered no clarifications in her memoirs, *Ma double vie*, and consequently a variety of conflicting accounts exists. Bernhardt sometimes celebrated her birthday on 23 October, although 22 October 1844 is the birthdate officially recorded in the *Dictionnaire de Biographie Française*, where her parentage is cited as the out-of-wedlock union between the Jewish courtesan, Julia Bernardt (*sic*) and the naval officer, Paul Morel, a native of Le Havre. Biographical sources also refer to Sarah's mother as Judith or Julie Van Hard and to her father as Edouard Bernhardt. Although discrepancies arise over whether her father belonged to the legal or naval professions, his French origins are never contested. On the other hand, the nationality of Madame Bernhardt (as she shall be named in this study, given her subsequent adoption of the famous surname) could have been Dutch or German. It is more than likely that Holland was her country of origin, particularly when one takes into account that rumours of a German ancestry tended to be fuelled by those who, at various points during Sarah's career, sought to bring the actress into disrepute by questioning her nationality and patriotism.

The exact details can probably never be known with certainty, but as Bernhardt would have been the first to insist, this is of little

1

consequence. What *is* clear is that Sarah-Rosine's illegitimate origins were far from auspicious, and her arrival would have been a less than welcome addition to her mother's irregular, courtesan lifestyle.

After her birth she was conveniently farmed out to a series of friends and relatives, then to boarding school and to the convent of Grand-Champs at Versailles. During these years, she received only rare visits from her butterfly mother. Contact with her father was also minimal and short-lived (he died abroad in 1857). Of necessity, Sarah's early nomadic years induced an unusual degree of self-reliance which would prove an invaluable resource throughout her stormy career. Her own account of her childhood and youth, in *Ma double vie*, however fictionalised through 'remembrance of things past', depicts an affectionate but lonely child, subject to violent fits of temper and *crises de nerfs*, which resulted in severe bouts of illness. These, too, were to be significant factors in both making and marring her theatrical career.

If Sarah had had her own way, she might have retreated from the world altogether into the cloistered life of a nun. Fortunately for us, her early passion for religious mysticism, fostered in the convent, was rapidly converted into a love of the theatre. Initially the conversion was brought about through the auspices of the Duc de Morny (half-brother of Louis Napoleon), who saw to it that Sarah obtained her entry to the Conservatoire. The Duc was just one of the many distinguished and artistic figures who moved in the *demi-monde* circle of Judith and her sister Rosine Berendt. During the Second Empire, an established courtesan could expect to thrive on a lively circle of well-to-do male admirers, the official bourgeois ideology of family values and respectability being more theoretical than actual. In this way, Sarah's disadvantaged origins actually worked in her favour, and on more than one occasion 'family connections' would be prevailed upon to further her career.

Sarah's determination to do things her own way was evident as soon as she began her dramatic training. At her audition for the Conservatoire, she discovered that there was no actor to give her the cues for the scene she had prepared as Agnès in *L'Ecole des femmes* and promptly departed from convention by offering, instead, a recitation of La Fontaine's fable *Les deux pigeons*. Even the

2

authority and reputation of her celebrated teachers – Provost, Samson and Régnier – did not overawe Bernhardt into a passive acceptance of their instruction, once her training was under way. In *Ma double vie*, for example, she describes how, at her own insistence (and contrary to Provost's wishes), she chose to present a scene from *Zaïre* for her first examination in tragedy.[2] Having been persuaded to fall in with her wishes, Provost then insisted that she play the chosen scene – in which Zaïre confronts her brother Nérestan – with a violent emphasis at the line 'Frappe! dis-je, je l'aime . . .', delivered as the heroine falls at Nérestan's feet. Sarah wanted to deliver the line with 'douceur' and 'résignation'. Finding herself overruled in class she rehearsed the scene as Provost requested, but when it came to the examination she played it her own way, receiving great applause and the second prize.

Sarah did badly in the second set of examinations, having had to transfer to Samson's classes shortly before the competition, owing to Provost's ill health. Her strong personality clearly clashed with Samson's 'authoritative and stubborn' character, and she considered the passages he chose for her comedy and tragedy examinations, both taken from works by Casimir Delavigne, as 'very bad scenes from two very bad plays'.[3] These examinations proved disastrous. No prize at all for tragedy – a performance as much marred by Bernhardt's dislike of her part as by her struggle with an unfortunate hairstyle, devised by her mother for the occasion – but in comedy she took second prize, deferring to the greater beauty of Marie Lloyd, who claimed first.

Despite the disappointing examination results, Sarah availed herself of the Duc de Morny and Camille Doucet, then Minister of Fine Arts, to secure a début at the Comédie Française. It proved, however, to be an unpromising beginning. Her first performance in Racine's *Iphigénie en Aulide* (August 1862) was quite unexceptional. The influential theatre critic Francisque Sarcey gave the newcomer a fleeting mention in *L'Opinion Nationale*, commenting only on her physique, the beauty of her face – 'notably its upper part' – and the 'clarity' of her diction.[4] Jules Huret in his biographical sketch (compiled from interviews with the actress) recalls the laughter which broke out as Sarah, at the moment of Iphigénie's sacrifice, raised her long, emaciated

3

arms.[5] In Sarah's own view, a well-proportioned body – 'a small head, a long neck, a short figure, and long arms and legs' – was one of the chief prerequisites for the actress; she did not consider great beauty to be essential.[6] Yet it was the fashionable beauty of the woman which so often captured the attention of audiences and critics, rather than the talent of the actress, and Sarah, whose physique was better suited to her art than was her looks, suffered from this superficial judgement. The laughter provoked by her physique on this occasion was a foretaste of the endless lampoons to which her mass of hair, slender figure and thin limbs would be subjected throughout her career.

Not only was Sarah disadvantaged in terms of physique, but her temperament also interrupted the development of her teenage talent on the national stage. Sarah's training had not provided sufficient discipline to combat her tempestuous nature, and a few months after her début roles, which consisted of a further two mediocre performances in *Valérie* and *Les Femmes savantes*, a ferocious contretemps with Comédie Française *sociétaire* Mme Nathalie resulted in her first, though by no means last, impromptu exit.

This was a potentially serious set-back to Bernhardt's determination to earn her own living and be independent of both her family and a husband. She had already refused the offer of a rich but elderly suitor, not giving in to family pressure exhorting her to accept a secure future and promising expectations. She did not, however, reject the influential intervention of those 'family connections' who had already acted effectively on her behalf by engineering her admission to the Conservatoire, and so a few days after leaving the Comédie, Bernhardt found herself engaged at the Théâtre du Gymnase (March 1863). On this occasion, she did not take her letter of engagement home to be stamped with the authority of her mother's signature, as she had done in the case of the Comédie contract, but announced to the Gymnase director, Montigny, that she would sign it herself: 'I am emancipated. . . so my own signature is valid' was her provocative challenge.[7]

Under the careful, caring and stabilising direction of the former actor Montigny, the Gymnase had become a home for much of the mid-century social drama. In particular, several plays by

Alexandre Dumas *fils* were produced there, beginning with *Diane de Lys* in 1853 which was followed by *Le Demi-monde*, his first *pièce à thèse*, in March 1855. If Bernhardt had remained at the Gymnase during the 1860s, she might have found herself playing in *L'Ami des femmes* (1864) or *Les Idées de Mme Aubray* (1867). However, Sarah's unremarkable period at the Gymnase was to be almost as short as her spell with the Comédie, and her triumphs in roles created by Dumas were to come much later in her career.

In a little less than a year after her Gymnase début, Sarah, now in characteristic style, left abruptly for Spain. In her memoirs, Sarah argues that this was due to her intense dislike of her latest role in Raymond Deslandes's 'stupid' play *Un mari qui 'lance sa femme* which opened in April 1864.[8] Her biographers, however, speculate on an episode in Sarah's life which she omits from her memoirs: her liaison with the Belgian nobleman, the Prince de Ligne, and the birth of her only child, Maurice. Accounts vary from an amicably terminated romance to a rupture on the scale and in the character of Armand and Marguerite in *La Dame aux Camélias*. Certainly, marriage would have been out of the question. An aristocrat of the Prince de Ligne's standing might take an actress for his mistress, but never for a wife – unless he wished to incur the unrelenting wrath of his relatives. For Sarah, the liaison and resulting single parenthood simply confirmed her 'outsider' status. The facts of her own illegitimacy, courtesan connections and the dishonourable status of her chosen profession were already more than sufficient to debar her from the ranks of bourgeois respectability. But it seems unlikely, in any case, that she would have desired admission.

In terms of Sarah's so far unpromising career, the pregnancy was to prove a notable interruption, though her disappearance from the stage was neither as lengthy nor as mysterious as Ellen Terry's six 'lost years'.[9] She returned to Paris soon after leaving it, having been given to understand that her mother was seriously ill. Once assured that the latter was out of any danger, Sarah set up home in the rue Duphot, accompanied by Régina, the youngest of her two sisters. Though Madame Bernhardt doted on her second daughter, Jeanne, she had little time for Régina and clashed constantly with Sarah. A separate residence resolved family frictions, gave Sarah her independence and provided a home for her son Maurice, born on 22 December 1864. Family friend and lifelong companion of Sarah, Mme Guérard (affectionately nicknamed *Mon petit'dame*) assisted in caring for the child, and gradually Sarah resumed her public profile. With a son to provide for, Sarah's need for work was more urgent than ever.

The following December (1865), during a visit to the Théâtre de la Porte Saint-Martin, Sarah was persuaded to act as an impromptu understudy for Mlle Debay in the principal role of a spectacular play, *La Biche au bois*. Though offered a contract at the Porte Saint-Martin, she had higher aspirations. Finally, with the aid and influence of Camille Doucet, she secured a contract at the Théâtre de l'Odéon, second only to the Comédie Française in reputation. The Odéon was then under the direction of Félix Duquesnel, who recognised Sarah's talent and engaged her despite the reservations of his partner, Chilly.

At the Odéon Sarah's apprenticeship began in earnest, and in August 1866 she embarked on a variety of roles in plays by Molière, Shakespeare, Racine and George Sand. Her contributions were noted with keen interest by the critics, and she earned the plaudits of some of the most eminent among them – especially Théophile Gautier and, at long last, Francisque Sarcey. As always, she cultivated an extravagant life style and could boast many friendships in high society. Of particular interest in relation to this period of Sarah's career is her contact with George Sand, just one of her many friendships with distinguished women. In her memoirs Sarah recalls the timidity and charm of the fêted French writer at the time of their initial acquaintance,[10] and George Sand, for her part, documents the progress of the rising theatrical star in some of her correspondence.[11] These glimpses of Sarah's formative years at the Odéon allow us, for once, to see Sarah through another woman's eyes.

In a letter to Duquesnel (30 May 1867), replying to queries concerning the casting of her play *Le Marquis de Villemer* which opened at the Odéon in July 1867, George Sand had been unable to comment on Sarah's suitability for the part of the Baronne d'Arglade, being unacquainted with the actress at this time. However, she indicated confidence in Duquesnel's proposal to nominate the actress of his choice, and this trust did not prove misplaced. During the summer of 1867, coinciding with a glittering and brilliant *Exposition Universelle*, Sarah in fact gave two performances in plays by Mme Sand. Following her appearance as the Baronne d'Arglade, she went on to play Mariette in *François le Champi* (August 1867), and Mme Sand wrote directly to Sarah (18 August 1867) to thank her for her affectionate letters and to congratulate her on having played the part 'comme un ange'. Eighteen months later George Sand was writing to Duquesnel and Chilly (20 February 1869) to recommend Sarah for the part of Hélène de Mérangis in her play *L'Autre*, which was eventually scheduled for production in February of the following year. Sarah must have already been toying with the idea of leaving the Odéon because George Sand records her apprehension lest Sarah might have left before the production. In the event, she was still available and was engaged for the part.

As to events and performances involving Sarah between *François le Champi* and *L'Autre*, George Sand's comments reveal a mixture of admiration, anxiety and a few misgivings. Sarah's performances could certainly vary from the downright mediocre (as Hortense in *Le Testament de César Girodot* by Adolphe Belot and Villetard, January 1868) to the magnetic (as Anna Damby in *Kean* by Alexandre Dumas *père*, February 1868). She was not wholly to blame for these fluctuations in the standard of her performances, as certain productions were clearly unworthy of her – or anybody's – abilities. An outstanding cast, for example, performed a translation of Shakespeare's *King Lear* in April 1868 with Sarah taking the part of Cordelia, but in the following month, players – including Sarah – were required to harness their talents to a poor satirical comedy, *La Loterie du mariage*, by Jules Barbier.

Sarah's key success at the Odéon was her *travesti* performance as the Florentine minstrel in the poet-turned-dramatist François Coppé's *Le Passant* (January 1869). It was a performance which won her the hearts of the Left Bank students. George Sand added her own accolade in a letter to her son Maurice (26 April 1869), declaring that the actress was more impressive than ever – though she also expressed concern for Sarah's health, referring to her skeletal physique and rumours of her having taken poison. Whatever the private disappointments and tribulations of Sarah's life at this time – and there have been many speculative varia-

tions on the themes of thwarted love and artistic misgivings –
there was worse to follow. A few months later, in a letter to her
daughter-in-law (11 September), Mme Sand wrote of the misfortunes of her actress, 'la fille aux catastrophes', whose residence,
16 rue Auber, had been gutted by a fire. Sarah, who was unin-
sured, found herself in pressing financial difficulties, though
fortunately the *prima donna* Adelina Patti gave a benefit performance on her behalf.

In September 1869 George Sand attended a performance of *Le
Bâtard* by Alfred Touroude, a drama reminiscent of *Le Fils naturel*
(1858) by Dumas *fils*. Writing once again to her daughter-in-law
(23 September 1869), she praised both play and players, including Sarah, who took the insignificant role of Jeanne and yet
succeeded, by all accounts, in making something out of nothing.
Mme Sand began to fear that the piece would prove a box-office
success, be given an extended run and thereby delay the presentation of her own play *L'Autre*, but she need not have worried on
that score. One more production preceded the latter: *L'Affranchi*,
by Latour de Saint-Ybars (January 1870). Writing to Gustave
Flaubert (19 January 1870), the authoress confided that Sarah
was 'très jolie' in her role as Bérénice in this production, though
she had no fears of this play postponing her own, as it was of very
poor quality overall.

Sand's correspondence in the period immediately prior to
*L'Autre* presents a view of Sarah which is coloured by the problems surrounding the production. Rehearsals had not been going
smoothly, owing to the disgruntled actress Adèle Page, who was
less than satisfied with what she considered to be the inferior role
of Jeanne Fayat. The petty jealousies and rivalry between Sarah
and Adèle prompted reproaches from the playwright, which
successfully provoked Sarah into giving a highly praised performance as the young and chaste Hélène. This pleased both the
critics (notably Théophile Gautier) and the author, who declared
the production an artistic and financial success.

In the wake of *L'Autre*, performances at the Odéon (as else-
where) were abruptly halted by the onset of the Franco-Prussian
war, and Paris rang with cries of 'A Berlin! à Berlin!'. Though
illness obliged Sarah to spend the outbreak of war at Eaux-
Bonnes, regaining her health – she was in a fragile, emaciated

and potentially consumptive condition – she returned to Paris for the duration of the siege. She now assigned herself a new role in the 'theatre of war' by turning the Odéon into a makeshift hospital and nursing the wounded. The Comte de Kératry, a former *habitué* of the courtesan milieu – acting as quarter-master during the siege – saw to it that Sarah had food supplies for her Odéon hospital. Sarah's recollections of the siege and bombardment (which take up several chapters in her memoirs) are coloured by a rather zealous, patriotic tone. This probably reflects a subsequent wish to dispel any uncertainty surrounding her allegiance and loyalty to France. For, as the end of the conflict drew near, she discovered to her horror that her immediate family, whom she thought to have placed safely in Le Havre, were in reality taking shelter on enemy soil. It would appear that Sarah's mother had decided to take the family to the relative safety of Homburg for the end of the war. As Paris collapsed and the Prussians scented victory, Sarah had to undertake a hazardous journey through enemy lines in order to be reunited with her family. Madame Bernhardt's temporary asylum in Germany fuelled conjectures regarding her German ancestry. Whether fact or fiction, the speculation gave those who resented the ascendant fortunes of the courtesan-actress the opportunity to question her loyalties. Her reaction at the time – as decades later at the outbreak of the First World War – was to repudiate the accusations by demonstrating her ardent patriotism. She would always consider herself a loyal subject of France and for many years made her position explicit by refusing to include Germany in her international tours.

Though Sarah returned to the capital with her family, she was forced to leave again during the struggles of the Commune, and while Paris burned, she looked on from her refuge in St Germain-en-Laye. Finally, after the fall of the Commune and the humiliating armistice which ensued, she re-entered the smouldering city to resume her work in the theatre. She opened at the Odéon in a one-act drama, *Jean-Marie* by André Theuriet (October 1871), which was later revived successfully in London. After further winter productions came her major resounding success as Doña Maria de Neubourg in Victor Hugo's *Ruy Blas*, early in 1872. The production became a rallying point for the

9

republican spirit, signalling the rekindling of national pride and morale. The end of the Second Empire, so powerfully captured in Zola's image of the dying Nana, spelt the end of a lascivious and corrupt régime. Hugo, who had recently been repatriated, became the literary exemplar of the Republic, the conscience of a new era. However deeply Sarah regretted the passing of the Empire, she ardently embraced the republican spirit and eagerly besought Duquesnel for the part of Hugo's Queen.

The author himself was to attend preparations for the production. Any initial antipathy towards the French poet, born of the prejudice and controversy he constantly attracted, was immediately assuaged during rehearsals; she was completely won over by his wit and charm. It was one of those rare, propitious moments in theatre history, when the play, the players and the public are all in accord. Above all, it was a personal triumph for Sarah. Whatever reservations critics had about certain aspects of the production, they had none when it came to assessing her own contribution. She was the undisputed star. Moreover, this success heralded her departure from the Odéon and her second début at the Comédie Française, whose director, Emile Perrin, was now anxious to lure the new box-office celebrity back to the National Theatre.

Though Sarah regretted leaving the Odéon, she did not disdain the promotion, distinction and increase in salary which the Comédie contract offered. Angered at losing his star, Chilly understandably sued Sarah for breach of the Odéon contract – the first of Sarah's lawsuits in the theatre, though by no means her last. Their friendship ended as it had begun, amid animosity and acrimony, cut short by Chilly's sudden death shortly after a banquet given in Hugo's honour to celebrate the one-hundredth performance of *Ruy Blas*.

Her new life at the Comédie Française was far from trouble-free. Bernhardt's headstrong, independent and mercurial disposition conflicted continually with the rigors of obeying the rules and harmonising with the national company. For her second début, in Dumas *père*'s *Mademoiselle de Belle-Isle* (November 1872), she gave a disappointing performance, due in part to anxiety for her mother, who was taken ill during the evening. But successes were to follow, notably in productions in which Sarah partnered the

10

handsome and talented actor Jean Mounet-Sully (who is generally cited as one of Sarah's many lovers). In the following month, opposite Mounet-Sully's Nero, she gave an acclaimed performance as Junie in Racine's *Britannicus*. Her slight, slender figure was admirably suited to the *travesti* role of Chérubin in Beaumarchais's *Le Mariage de Figaro*, which she played in January of the following year, but she was ridiculously miscast in her next part, as the wicked princess in Octave Feuillet's *Dalila* (March 1873).

Sarah's difficulties and erratic performances were brought about, to some extent, by her clashes with Perrin. The director was rather alarmed by the headstrong actress he had engaged and constantly reacted to Sarah's demands by opposing her wishes. Mutiny was punished by less interesting roles, the more substantial parts being appropriated by Sophie Croizette, who was as compliant as Sarah was rebellious. The two actresses were total opposites, even in physique — Croizette's plump, sanguine figure contrasting sharply with Bernhardt's thin frame and sorrowful brow. Though friendship existed between these two, rivalry would flare up during productions, and rehearsals were often stormy. In Octave Feuillet's *Le Sphinx*, staged in March 1874, Sarah was landed with the dull, insipid part of Berthe de Savigny, while Croizette was cast in the key role of the *femme fatale*, Blanche de Chelles. Bernhardt describes in her memoirs how, during rehearsals for this production, she set about upstaging Croizette.[12] In the third act, when Berthe discovers her husband and Blanche kissing by moonlight, Bernhardt insisted on having flattering moonlight effects to enhance her own entry. Despite Perrin's objections, Sarah eventually had her own way and her own special lighting. A similar problem arose in the later production of *L'Etrangère* by Dumas *fils* (February 1876) in which the playwright had promised Sarah the principal role of Catherine de Septmonts. But when it came to the casting, Sarah was given the shorter role of the mysterious foreigner Mistress Clarkson; the part of Catherine went to Croizette. An indignant Sarah was forced to acquiesce but turned the tables yet again by outclassing and upstaging the unfortunate Croizette.

Try as he might, Perrin was powerless to limit Sarah's increasing autonomy in matters of interpretation. One proof of her unerring instincts in this area came with her appearance as

Phèdre, on 21 December 1874, in a production mounted to commemorate Racine's birthday. Previously, at the Odéon in August 1866 and then at the Comédie in September 1873, she had essayed the role of Aricie, but this was a far cry from the demands and range of Racine's eponymous heroine. Furthermore, any actress braving this part invited inevitable comparisons with Rachel Félix. It was the role which had been the pinnacle of Rachel's all too brief (she died of a tubercular condition at the age of 38) but brilliant career in the first half of the nineteenth century. Consequently, her interpretation of the part was widely regarded as the bench-mark for subsequent readings. Yet Bernhardt proved herself equal to her predecessor's acclaimed Phèdre and played to an enthusiastic full house. Mounet-Sully again shared in Sarah's success, complementing her performance with a splendid Hippolyte. They repeated their triumphant partnership in revivals of two plays by Hugo which had become firm favourites in the new wave of republicanism: in November 1877 Sarah played Doña Sol in *Hernani* (with Mounet-Sully in the title role), and in *Ruy Blas* (April 1879) she once again appeared as the Queen. Sarah thought that Mounet-Sully's Ruy Blas was a hundred times better than Lafontaine's interpretation in the Odéon production.[13] They were clearly favourites with the audiences who enjoyed the spectacles of tragic love, spiced with speculations of an off-stage romance. Perrin was quick to exploit the box-office potential of the partnership, and when in the production of Parodi's *Rome vaincue* (September 1876), Bernhardt turned down the role of the young and tragic victim Opimia and insisted instead on playing the old blind woman Posthumia, he had to cast Mounet-Sully in the role of the old idiot Vestaepor, as an effective counterpart to the chosen role of the actress.[14]

Perrin was reluctant to allow Sarah lengthy breaks from her work at the Comédie, either because he was unwilling to forfeit the presence of his principal audience attraction, or else, purely and simply, he was attempting to exert his shrinking authority over an actress who refused to be subjugated. Thus, in the summer of 1874, when Sarah desperately wanted time out to recover from exhausted nerves and the delicate health which still plagued her, he insisted she remain to perform her examination

12

role of Zaïre. Sarah complied on this occasion, and her interpretation of Voltaire's heroine brought fresh public acclaim. Before her undertaking of Phèdre, however, she did manage to snatch a restful vacation in Brittany. Not only had her tendency to neurasthenia been exacerbated by the exhausting demands of performance, but the recent death of her sister Régina had also added to her low spirits. During the period of her sister's decline (at Sarah's residence in the rue de Rome), the actress had adopted the eccentric and macabre habit of sleeping in a specially designed rosewood coffin at Régina's bedside – another episode which furthered her notoriety.

The mid-1870s was a period of loss and suffering for Sarah. Régina's death was shortly followed by that of Madame Bernhardt whose precarious state of health finally gave out in May 1876. In addition, 1876 also saw the death of her erstwhile friend of the Odéon days, George Sand, whose years of prolific writing had come to a close just as Sarah's acting career was reaching unprecedented heights.

As an antidote to ill-health, increasing depression and the frustration engendered by her relations with Perrin (who persisted in casting her in inappropriate or unrewarding roles), Sarah sought other outlets for her creative energies. She tried her hand at sculpting, taking a studio near the Place de Clichy, and became a pupil of the sculptor Mathieu Meusnier. A bust of Régina was shown at the Salon of 1875, the first of several pieces to be exhibited, many modelled after Sarah's friends. Not everyone warmed to her new artistic endeavour; Perrin resented the time and energy she expended on this latest venture, and among accredited sculptors, Rodin is quoted as saying, 'the bust is rubbish and the public is stupid to linger over it'.[15] Undaunted by adverse criticism, Sarah also learned to paint. Her circle of admirers included the artists Louise Abbéma and Georges Clairin, with whom she was to enjoy life-long friendships. Both produced portraits of Sarah for the 1876 Salon. It was Georges Clairin – reputed to be another of Sarah's lovers – who, in collaboration with several other artists, had a hand in the interior design and decoration of the sumptuous residence which Sarah (at the close of 1875) had built at the corner of the Avenue de Villiers and the rue Fortuny. The architect was Félix Escalier, and the house was to become a *lieu de réunion* for Sarah's numerous friends and acquaintances (not to mention her menagerie of exotic animals).

By now Sarah featured constantly in society gossip columns, always attracting attention and creating news. Her rise to fame had been well-timed. She had erratically but successfully managed to launch her acting career by means of the courtesan circles. After 1871 this would not have been possible, as French society, recovering its dignity, morality and national pride, saw the courtesan as a scapegoat for much of the lascivious behaviour of the pre-war era. Many of the Second Empire courtesans had been able to use the theatre as a means of staging their beauty and attracting wealthy lovers in whom they invested their future careers. Sarah might well have trodden this path, had she not discovered a talent and passion for the theatre which had been sufficiently developed and established before the disruption and chaos of war. Nevertheless, connotations of the *demi-monde*, out of which she had risen to fame and fortune, would never leave her. Rather than attempt to live them down, Sarah chose instead to flaunt her disregard for the hypocritical, newly-found, *bourgeois* respectability by furthering an image of notoriety. She had an enormous appetite for work and for the company of friends and lovers. Her life was a whirlwind of artistic and social engagements, and she was rarely alone, rarely idle and rarely out of the public eye.

Yet her self-created personality cult grew increasingly at odds with the traditional ethos of the Comédie Française, which emphasised the subordination of the individual artist to the ensemble as a whole. Her unorthodox, some would say immoral, off-stage life style was incompatible with the image of respectability denoted by the national playhouse. As Sarah insisted more and more on turning her 'private' life into a public spectacle and, as an actress, encoded passion and exotica in her stage image, so Perrin increasingly found his new star impossible to control and to keep within the confines and constraints of Comédie policy.

The growing tension between Sarah and Perrin came to a head in two incidents which occurred shortly before the proposed visit of the company to London in the summer of 1879. The first of these was Sarah's ascent in M. Giffard's hot air balloon, when she

14

flew over both Paris and Perrin, who went purple with rage as she sailed above him, showing a flagrant disregard for Comédie etiquette and decorum.[16] Sarah subsequently recorded the exploit in a piece of fantasy prose, *Dans les nuages: impressions d'une chaise* (1878).[17] The second irritant for Perrin arose when Sarah announced her intention to give drawing-room performances during the London season, a money-making scheme that had been proposed to her by the impresario William Jarrett, who later engineered her American tours. An outraged Comédie Française retaliated by attempting to leave Sarah out of the tour, but the managers of the London season, Mayer and Hollingshead, threatened to cancel if Bernhardt, Mounet-Sully or Croizette failed to appear. Perrin consequently withdrew his threat and proffered an olive branch by making Sarah a fully-fledged member of the Comédie Française, an honour which he also bestowed on Croizette at the same time.

Thus we see Sarah on the eve of the first of many regular visits to London. She was in her mid-thirties and was already a star, but years of international fame and a lifetime's service to the theatre still lay ahead. The tensions and frictions which had characterised her stay at the Comédie made continuing membership in the company increasingly dubious and thus, paradoxically, were factors in determining her future international career. She had provoked and enraged her fellow professionals, fellow artists, the French press and, in some respects, the Parisian public itself, to a degree which would shortly lead to her second rupture with the Comédie and to a new phase in her career. The London visit of 1879 heralded a new era; for while Paris was torn between glorification of Sarah's dramatic achievements on the one hand and outrage at her private exploits on the other, the English capital awaited with unreserved enthusiasm 'the greatest feminine personality. . . that France had known since Joan of Arc'.[18]

# Notes

1. Quoted in, Lysiane Bernhardt, *Sarah Bernhardt: ma grand' mère* (Paris: Editions du Pavois, 1945), p. 21. Unless otherwise stated, translations from French texts are my own.
2. Sarah Bernhardt *Ma Double vie: mémoires de Sarah Bernhardt*, 2 vols (Paris: Bibliothèque Charpentier, 1923 edn), vol. 1, p. 97.
3. Sarah Bernhardt, *Mémoires*, vol. 1, p. 104.
4. Ibid., p. 132.
5. Jules Huret, *Sarah Bernhardt: acteurs et actrices d'aujourd' hui* (Paris: Juven, 1899), p. 17.
6. Sarah Bernhardt, *L'Art du théâtre* (Paris: Nilsson, 1923), p. 40.
7. Sarah Bernhardt, *Mémoires*, vol. I, p. 143.
8. Ibid., p. 144.
9. Bernhardt's contemporary, Ellen Terry, likewise adjourned her career in the late 1860s and disappeared from theatrical life for six years, during which time she gave birth to two illegitimate children.
10. Sarah Bernhardt, *Mémoires*, vol. I, p. 170.
11. The letters by George Sand referred to in this chapter are taken from her collected *Correspondance* (Paris: Garnier, 1964–). Letters cited are from vol. XX (June 1866 – May 1868) and vol. XXI (June 1868 – March 1870).
12. Sarah Bernhardt, *Mémoires*, vol. II, pp. 35–6.
13. Ibid., p. 87.
14. Ibid., pp. 70–1.
15. Quoted in, G.-J. Geller, *Sarah Bernhardt* (Paris: Gallimard, 1931), p. 110.
16. Sarah Bernhardt, *Mémoires*, vol. II, p. 77.
17. In the tale, written from the chair's point of view, Sarah appears in the guise of Doña Sol. The idea of writing an account from the point of view of an inanimate object was a literary fad in vogue at the time.
18. Thérèse Berton, *Sarah Bernhardt as I Knew Her: The Memoirs of Mme Pierre Berton as told to Basil Woon* (London: Hurst & Blackett, 1923), p. 209.

# 2 Classical Overtures

On arrival at Folkestone, Sarah was greeted by a crowd of enthusiastic English admirers, eager to catch sight of the much-discussed French actress. Among those there to welcome her were the handsome, Hamlet-like actor, Forbes Robertson, and the writer, socialite and eventual friend of Bernhardt's, Oscar Wilde. A bouquet from Henry Irving awaited her at her London residence in Chester Square, though this was small compensation for the comparatively dismal entry into London itself, via a gloomy and unwelcoming Charing Cross Station. True, there was a red carpet down on the platform, but this had served earlier for the Prince and Princess of Wales who had, ironically, just left for the French capital. Though disappointed by the city's low-key welcome, Sarah's spirits rallied as the press besieged Chester Square, and London society began to open hospitable doors.

The inaugural night of the company's season was 2 June 1879. In the original schedule of productions, Bernhardt was not to perform in the opening programme, which consisted of a Molière double bill, with Croizette taking the part of Célimène in *Le Misanthrope*. The combined factors of impatient curiosity on the part of her audience and Bernhardt's unwillingness to make her début on the London stage as Dumas's Mistress Clarkson, as planned, resulted in a last minute alteration: the second act of *Phèdre* was added to the programme, wedged between the two full-length productions.

As in France, the earlier performances of Rachel in this role were much discussed. An expectant audience of connoisseurs, drawn from the ranks of the fashionable and educated middle classes (sufficiently trained in the art of the French language and the classics to be able to comprehend the gist of Phèdre's tragic story) eagerly awaited the opportunity to see how Bernhardt's performance would compare with that of her predecessor. It was an ambitious undertaking to offer the second act of Racine's tragedy in isolation. Though on the one hand it provided the actress with a vehicle for an emotional display demanding the

17

utmost exercise of technique and sensibility, on the other it involved the risk of failing to reach the pitch of tragic intensity normally achieved by playing the drama in its entirety. Such a failure would have left her with the task of deferring her conquest of the English public until another occasion.

Paradoxically, a fit of stage-fright worked to Bernhardt's advantage. Overcome by nerves at the moment of her entrance, Phèdre's suffering – as she recollected in *L'Art du théâtre* – was 'all too real'.[1] The tension generated by nerves produced the frenzied state which would otherwise have been reached only through the build-up of the first act. (Bernhardt suffered from stage-fright throughout her career. She identified two kinds: one which 'paralysed' and one which 'maddened'.[2] Fortunately, on this occasion it was the maddening variety which took hold and provided the impetus for a display of tragic suffering.)

As the moment came for Bernhardt to make her entrance, an audible hush fell on the auditorium of the Gaiety Theatre. Finally, as the love-stricken, guilty Phèdre appeared, majestic anguish was immediately visible in Sarah's facial expressions of agony, the disarray of her hair and the desperation communicated by the wild gesturing of her long arms, left bare amid folds of classical white drapery. Though 'Opera-Glass', the reviewer for *Era*, noted that she was 'a little worn and tired',[3] in general there was no hint that her tortured appearance in the role arose from any consideration other than her conception of the character. Nor, indeed, did she come across as nervous. Initially, some suspected that her evident frailty and fragility would be an obstacle to meeting the demands of the part, but as her performance progressed, it became clear that this was undoubtedly not the case. Bernhardt's Phèdre fused fragility and vulnerability with the energy and passion of a woman tortured by love. It was the emphasis on femininity in her conception which enraptured audience and critics alike. Writing after the full-length production of *Phèdre* later in the summer season, the *Daily Telegraph* reviewer commented:

> The new Phèdre never ceases to be a woman, a creature of intense feeling, a representative of resistless passion. Mark how she shows this absorption with Hippolyte – not with the tiger-spring of determina-

tion and resolve, not with the cruelty of baffled possession, but with a languishing hunger that is directly authorised by the text. When she opens her arms, and with a voice of caressing softness declares her weakness and her shame, it is the woman in Phèdre that speaks, the woman capable of unutterable tenderness and melting affection.[4]

Though highlighting the feminine was a feature of many of Bernhardt's heroines (whether ancient or modern), in the case of Racinian heroines it was a conception which the actress drew directly from her own reading of the playwright's tragic world and victims. In *L'Art du théâtre*, Bernhardt contrasts the heroines of Corneille – which she felt she could not play because they had 'minds' but not 'hearts' – with Racine's tragic heroines, whom she describes as universal and timeless: 'women who remain women beneath their heroism'.[5] It is not hard to understand Sarah's attraction to the world of Racinian tragedy, which focuses on female anguish, as opposed to Corneille's tragic universe of male valour and glory. Moreover, among Racine's women, it was Phèdre who for Bernhardt was 'the most touching, the most pure, the most sad victim of love',[6] and this provides the key to her interpretation. Sarah's acting style, which relied on the pathos of externalising the inner emotions, resulted in a pathetic, passionate and pictorial discourse, in contrast to the statuesque, restrained style of Rachel in the classics. Consequently, the critics pronounced that this was not the 'sombre grandeur' of Rachel's Phèdre but concurred that, if Bernhardt's Phèdre was less 'terrible and intense', Rachel's conception had been 'less womanlike, less sympathetic, less *entrainante*, than the Phèdre of Sarah Bernhardt'.[7] Where Rachel had inspired fear and awe, Bernhardt evoked sympathy and pity. The womanliness of her interpretation was not without a seductive 'serpentine grace', and as 'Opera-Glass' perceptively pointed out, 'the hunger of the passion of Sarah Bernhardt belongs to the school of Burne Jones, Rossetti, and Swinburne, and her agonised look, half shame, and half craving, affects me in the same way as do the pictures and poems of the artists I have quoted'.[8] The Rossettian, Pre-Raphaelite beauty of an erring but redeemable woman was encoded in her image of the languishing, dishevelled queen in whom guilt, pity and redemption were inextricably intertwined.

19

More than one critic commented that consequently it seemed as though Hippolyte (played by Mounet-Sully), through his coldness, was the transgressor, rather than the queen, through her ardour.

The climax of act two, as performed by Bernhardt, was undoubtedly the moment when, overcome by despair, Phèdre offers her breast for Hippolyte to strike a fatal blow and then, in turn, snatches his dagger, her thoughts turning to self-destruction. Repeatedly reviewers commented on this moment, which 'excited strongly the imagination of the spectators', and on the 'feeling of relief' which accompanied the applause as the curtain fell.[9] Audience response to Bernhardt's Phèdre demonstrates the success of her histrionic style of acting, which compelled the spectator to share in the emotion generated by the performer's total absorption in and identification with the role – the antithesis of the Coquelin school of anti-emotionalism and its advocacy of restraint and distance between actor and character. This latter approach was firmly embodied in the Conservatoire training, but was a tradition which Sarah typically worked against. Her use of a style based on sensibility held an immediate attraction for her London audiences, who seemed to delight in suffering along with her unfortunate heroine.

As a result of the tensions and frictions which arose subsequently in the summer season (caused as ever by Sarah's less than harmonious position in the company), augmenting prejudicial notes of dissension appeared in the reviews of Bernhardt's performances, and some critics went so far as to consider her emotionalist style as an unqualified failure. Notably, the *Pall Mall Gazette* took an anti-Bernhardt stance in its summary of the actress's method, claiming that she 'does not play her parts, she plays with them; and her personality is seldom hidden for more than a speech's length'.[10] Despite Sarah's advocacy of emotionalism, there is no denying that her own brand of femininity was curiously stamped on each of her womanly interpretations. In terms of voice, movement and style, Sarah's total identification with her part was coloured with her own peculiar brand of femininity and exotica, a combination which, over the years, would produce both fervent admiration and vehement criticism. In 1879, however, the critical voice of a few did little to deter the audiences who flocked to the Gaiety to be transfixed and transformed by the Bernhardt magnetism and magic.

At the end of June, Bernhardt offered the London theatre audiences another classical role, this time as the forlorn and heart-broken Andromaque. The spectacle of the grieving, black-veiled Trojan widow contrasted sharply with the image of the passionate Phèdre, shrouded in white drapery. To Andromaque, Bernhardt brought those broad and graceful gestures of supplication she had developed in *Phèdre*, prompting some critics to suggest that perhaps they 'were very much the same in the one part as in the other'.[11] 'Opera-Glass' in the *Era* stated that, though reviewers might continue to debate whether Sarah's was a sufficiently commanding presence when rendering a 'passage of tremendous tragic force', they could not but fail to acknowledge her consummate portrayal of the 'limpness and despondency of grief':

> In the poetry of grief and dejected "'haviour of the visage" she is unequalled. It was a realisation of one of those classical figures that weep on tombstones over an urn, a bit of wedgewood realised. The long lank arms, the black and mournful drapery, and the infinitely pathetic face leave a picture on the memory that cannot be readily effaced.[12]

Several reviewers were struck by the Greek spirit of her interpretation and especially her manner of adopting sculptural poses and attitudes to denote anguish, despair or grief, as the role required. As such, it was reminiscent of the technique of the Italian actress Adelaide Ristori, whose emotionalist style of 'picture acting' had captivated London audiences in the 1850s. Whereas Ristori possessed a physique which matched her larger-than-life manner of playing, however, one attraction of Bernhardt's stage presence lay in the contrast between the sheer power of her acting and the slightness of her physical build, between the portrayal of awesome heroism and the abiding image of tenderness. This opposition was captured in the supreme moment of her *Andromaque*, the crystallisation of the tragic dilemma in which she faces either the death of her son or the defilement of her husband's memory:

> The manner in which this is seized upon and turned to instant account speaks at once the power and insight of the actress. After a cry,

21

startled, passionate, and harrowing, she recoils with gestures of indescribable horror; then, with a mad appeal to one whose nobility she knows, as well as she knows and dreads his fatal love, she throws herself at his feet in an agony of appeal as though she would kiss the dust beneath his sandals. In this presentation of utter abandonment, in which all is turbulent, impetuous, unreasoning, all is yet beautiful in outline and matchless in grace.[13]

It was widely thought that the role of Andromaque did not afford enough scope for Bernhardt's special genius as a tragedienne. There were those who would have preferred to see her essay the part of Hermione, as Rachel had done. However, the more demanding role, on this occasion, was played by the young actress Mlle Dudlay, whose rendering of the part was too rhetorical and gestural for the English critics, although a few of them did detect a note of promise. Consequently, it was Mounet-Sully's Oreste who attracted more interest and carried away a greater share of plaudits.

Though English audiences found *Andromaque* a more taxing tragedy than *Phèdre*, given its greater diffusion of dramatic focus, even more difficulty was experienced with Voltaire's *Zaïre*. A receptive attitude towards the style and composition of Voltaire's tragedy was effectively blocked in advance by a condemnation of the play which came from a surprising quarter. The French critic Francisque Sarcey, lecturing to a gathering in London immediately prior to the production of Voltaire's tragedy, censured the folly of offering a play that was, in his view, but a poor imitation of *Othello* to audiences of Shakespeare's countrymen. Some English reviewers were less inclined to damn. Joseph Knight prefaced his comments on the play by observing that '*Zaïre* is better than its reputation',[14] and the reviewer for the *Morning Post* claimed that the play, although 'frigid in versification', deserved more credit than Sarcey gave it.[15]

Nevertheless, for Bernhardt enthusiasts the role of Zaïre was not one which afforded the actress opportunity to display her unique gifts. The critic for *The Times* found her delivery in the first act monotonous and the scene of her conversion in the second lacking in tragic intensity. He was more impressed by the climax of the third act, where Zaïre offers her life to her brother, yet even here felt that Bernhardt did not rise fully to the dramatic challenge the scene afforded. As for the concluding death scene, he found this disappointingly perfunctory.[16] The problem lay not only with the composition of Voltaire's tragedy (its conflicting Classical and pre-Romantic elements and the relatively limited role assigned to the tragic heroine-victim) but also with Bernhardt's ill-health and visible fatigue. Throughout the performance, given on 17 June, she was plagued by a cough which notably affected the delivery of her lines. The only redeeming quality of the production lay in the scenes which provided opportunity for the expression of Zaïre's passion for Orosmane, a passion at once all-consuming and innocent, in the delivery of which, it was recognised that Bernhardt had once again proved herself incomparable.

After *Zaïre* it was with great anticipation that the English public awaited the opportunity to see the Hugo productions which had caused such a sensation across the channel. As it was as much political change as dramatic taste which had brought Hugo back into vogue after the Franco-Prussian War, the passage of these Romantic dramas to another culture was inevitably problematical. Reaction to *Hernani* – the first production in the Gaiety season (9 June 1879) – ranged from lukewarm interest in the play itself to the *Spectator*'s unequivocal view that it was 'one of the very worst plays that was ever put upon a stage, and perhaps quite the most wearisome'.[17] For the audience and the majority of critics, a more tolerant view prevailed in which appreciation of the actual performances (and especially Bernhardt's) was paramount. As the reviewer for *The Times* wrote, 'for the bulk of the audience . . ., *Hernani* was Doña Sol, or rather Sarah Bernhardt. It is the actress who on this occasion gives importance and interest to the part, not the part to the actress'.[18]

In fact the dramatic potential of the role of Doña Sol is extremely limited. During the first four acts of this five-act drama there is little stage business for the performer to be actively engaged in, given that Doña Sol is depicted as a powerless woman, besieged by three suitors; she is a beautiful love object who cannot influence the destiny of her passion which, if free, would choose Hernani. Apart from languishing in exaggerated attitudes of affliction, there is little scope for the actress prior to the last act. Yet even within the limitations of the role in these

23

acts, which could furnish no real measure of Bernhardt's talent and resources, the actress nevertheless succeeded in projecting an image of enchanting and desirable femininity: 'In Doña Sol she is all the part permits her to be,' remarked *The Times* critic, 'A wonderfully graceful figure, beautifully dressed, picturesque pose, fair of face, loving of look, feminine of gesture, sweet of voice – admirably fitted, in a word, for what she has chiefly to do, which is to receive the full rush of love of three men'.[19]

Though suffering from the throat infection which was to prove even more troublesome in the production of *Zaïre*, the 'golden voice' for which she was renowned still held spectators spellbound. 'Melting', 'liquid', 'spoken music' were typical descriptions of her amorous speeches. These were given the fullest and most poignant interpretation in the fifth act of *Hernani* – by far the most interesting from the point of view of interpretative possibilities and dramatic interest. Briefly, the dénouement transforms the short-lived but idyllic marriage of Hernani and Doña Sol into a suicide pact, as the lovers are plunged into catastrophe by the peripeteian return of Don Ruy Gomez who comes to claim Hernani's death. It is Doña Sol who shows a reluctant Hernani the way to die. At this point, as the actress is called upon to portray a tableau of rapidly shifting emotions, as she gradually comes to recognise the inevitability of the lovers' fate, Sarah was able to seize the opportunity for fully developing her portrayal of modern passion. The Bernhardt electricity flowed, as the image of cloying femininity gave way to the highly charged portrait of a passionate woman guided to death by her ardour. Sarah's histrionic performance style swept her into a whirlwind of passion that seemed, at times, to border on delirium. Such energy and power emanated from her frail body that they threatened to tax the emotional resources of actress and audience almost beyond endurance. The scene was recounted in the reviews the following day; typical is the detail provided by the *Morning Post*:

In this crisis it is that the supreme power of art and the supreme sway of passion are shown as the present generation has not seen them shown. With her entire body, which seems to magnify itself for the purpose, she shelters her lover from the menace in that dry and burning eye. With a bound of indescribable and scarcely human impetuosity she throws herself upon him, and while her entire frame is between him and a danger she must regard as physical, she stretches out her hands and draws his head backwards, into her embrace, printing delirious kisses upon it. Now in the agony of intercession she crawls in abject terror at the feet of her slayer, now triumphantly she drinks her share of the poison she snatches from the hands of her husband, and shows him the way to death he may not evade. It is difficult to say which is the more remarkable, the absolutely electrical passion and the bursts like those of some wild animal, or the ineffable contentment and the divine rapture of her dying *pose*.[20]

That reviewers again emphasised the communication of this passion to the audience (who seemed to be suffering from a kind of nervous exhaustion by the end of the act) was further evidence of the charismatic persuasiveness of Sarah's emotionalist style. Inevitably there were isolated protests on the part of some who felt the spectacle to be artificial and meretricious. Just as the critic of the *Spectator* had stigmatised the play, so he dismissed Bernhardt's performance as an exercise in how to 'express physical exhaustion and the last depths of mental *ennui*, and to look as much like a half-witted person as possible'.[21] Accusations of artificiality, though not perhaps entirely without foundation, were greatly exaggerated. Gerda Taranow's erudite, fascinating and exhaustive study of Bernhardt's art of acting, has already exposed the contradictions between her advocacy of the emotionalist school and her calculated recourse to technique.[22] Yet in successful performances, even if the actress depended upon technique to reproduce emotion, it was invariably perceived and shared by the audience as genuine sensibility. The apparent paradox was implicitly resolved in the words of 'Opera Glass', reviewing Hernani: 'I hear that Sarah Bernhardt's style is artificial, that her attitudes are affected, and that her voice is harsh. Then I admire such artificiality, affectation, and harshness. Let those who have not seen Doña Sol go and judge for themselves'.[23]

At the end of June came Sarah's Odéon triumph, *Ruy Blas*. Compared to *Hernani*, English audiences, contrary to expectation, found the production disappointing. Criticism was directed both at the play and at the performances. The opportunity for Sarah to display her dramatic genius was even more restricted in *Ruy Blas*

25

than in *Hernani*, particularly because she did not have her own death scene. Furthermore, for those who had seen Frédéric Lemaître in the original title role or Charles Fechter in the English version, Mounet-Sulley's Ruy Blas was highly inadequate and judged by some to be an outright failure.

Despite the theatrical limitations of her role, Sarah partially, at least, managed to redeem the production by her portrait of the young queen, stifled and bored by Spanish court etiquette. She invested the role of the trapped queen with a remote, languorous and dreamlike quality. Even her magnificent costume echoed the theme of imprisonment: 'Her superb dress, rustling with precious stones and rigid with embroidery, was, in itself, almost a prison, and the stiff collar and the ruff held in something like bonds the slender, dainty neck.'[24] As in Bernhardt's conception of the Racinian heroine, it is the woman trapped beneath the shell of the queen who breaks free and deposes her regal self. In the final moments of *Ruy Blas* she is reduced to a

> poor broken creature, who, through her vain parade of pride, has seen her lover ruin his life, and who then, forgetful of rank, snatches his head in her hands, pulls it to her breast, and kisses the lips on which the last sigh of life is flickering, is a poor discrowned mortal with scarcely more life than the man who dies for her and in her clasp.[25]

Hence, Sarah's portrait of the queen brought close to death incited empathy and pity, and her musically cadenced delivery fell on receptive ears, all of which compensated the audience for the lack of whirlwind emotion characteristic of the heroine's tragedy in *Hernani*.

From the Comédie's repertory of modern plays, Bernhardt gave just two performances: as Mistress Clarkson in *L'Etrangère* and as Berthe de Savigny in *Le Sphinx*. *L'Etrangère* was to have been her first London production until it was replaced by the extract from *Phèdre* in the inaugural programme. A reading of Dumas's rather unorthodox critique of marriage and society reveals why Bernhardt did not consider her part promising material for the opening night. For it is only in the third act, in which Mistress Clarkson explains to Catherine de Septmonts her origins and background, revealing the cause of her antipathy towards the male sex and her condemnation of social hypocrisy, that there was fitting scope for Bernhardt's accomplishments. Furthermore, the mysterious outsider – the catalyst for Dumas's critique – is conceived as quite the opposite of a passionate woman. Her head firmly rules her heart, and she is not given to emotional display.

Unusual in its composition, the play was as much an intriguing puzzle for English audiences in the summer of 1879 as it had been for audiences at the Comédie in 1876. The London public had encountered the work in a translation recently performed at the Haymarket Theatre, and this paved the way for the reception of the original. As to Bernhardt's contribution to the performance, it was, to say the least, undertaken in unpropitious circumstances. After her draining performance in the second act of *Phèdre*, she had been reduced to a state of collapse, as well as suffering a loss of voice through the vomiting of blood. Sarah's commitment to her punishing schedules meant that she would always lay herself open to physical suffering and voice strain. This in turn created the opportunity for her critics to claim illness as a pretext for a poor performance, though it is clear that for much of her career, Sarah frequently drove herself into states of nervous exhaustion. In this instance, she was obviously at the mercy of Perrin's wish to exploit his box-office attraction and her own desire to conquer the English public. Sarah's insistence on performing is typical of her determination to succeed against all odds.

So it was that, despite medical opinion advising against further appearances, Bernhardt went ahead with *L'Etrangère*. She was drugged with opium and performed in a trance-like state, disastrously cutting a large part of Mistress Clarkson's narrative in the third act as a result of her condition. Yet this seemed to go unnoticed by reviewers, to judge by their accounts of the performance. Praise for Bernhardt's conception of the bewitching and mysterious siren-figure was unanimous. In the *Daily Telegraph*, the reviewer tried to isolate the salient features of her technique in the first act, in order to penetrate the magnetism emanating from the actress:

What is there in this most graceful and elegant figure, in these thin, expressive features, and in the snake-like movement of the artist, that

27

causes such a glow of satisfaction and pleasure? Is it the voice so exquisitely musical? Is it the marvellous expression of the eyes that soften and penetrate at one glance? Is it the admirable composure and faultless elegance as this artistic mystery commands the scene? Or what is it that makes the surrounding picture fade into mist at the approach of this calm and slow-moving figure?[26]

Reference to Bernhardt's 'snake-like' movement identifies the characteristically undulating, seductive body gestures which she later developed in the portrayal of such *femme fatale* creations as Cleopatra. Many of her costumes were designed to accentuate her serpentine movements, with folds of drapery which hugged the contours of her body, whirling out behind her in trains of fabric. Her costuming in *L'Etrangère* was no exception. In the third act she appeared 'in a dress of fairly Oriental luxury that might absolutely have come out of the "Arabian Nights"'.[27] The *Spectator*, though more positive about *L'Etrangère* than *Hernani*, nevertheless expressed its approval in backhanded compliments, stating, on the question of physique and attire, that 'Sarah Bernhardt overcomes certain physical defects with remarkable skill, she drapes an attenuated form with equal taste and success, and she uses her arms, which are too long and too lank, with much grace and expressiveness.'[28]

Among the more positive reviewers, interest concentrated on the third act. The sense of purity emanating from the delicately built woman on stage, even as she rehearses shadowy deeds from earlier life, truly harmonised with the image of a *Vierge du Mal*, as a disappointed suitor had once christened Mistress Clarkson. During the biographical narration Bernhardt demonstrated her command of stagecraft, constantly varying her movements and making full use of the performance space in order to sustain dramatic interest. She gave her account 'on three different parts of the stage to avoid monotony', made 'use now of a twisted handkerchief, now of a fan of feathers, to suggest ease, to suppress passion, or to avoid grief'.[29] In this way, Bernhardt's scene with the Duchess was as diverse and passionate as the most ardent of her love scenes in the classical drama.

Octave Feuillet's *Le Sphinx*, given on 14 June 1879, was as big a failure as *L'Etrangère* was a success. The critics considered the drama an inept and vulgar play, supposing its only attraction for

# God's Message to All

## The Gospel - God's provision for your Salvation

"I want to remind you of the gospel...by this gospel you are saved...that CHRIST DIED for our sins according to the Scriptures, that HE WAS BURIED, that HE WAS RAISED on the third day according to the Scriptures." *I Corinthians 15:1-4*

"We all, like sheep, have gone astray; each of us has turned to his own way; AND THE LORD HAS LAID ON HIM the iniquity of us all." *Isaiah 53:6*

"HE IS THE ATONING SACRIFICE for our sins: and not only for ours but also for the sins of the whole world." *1 John 2:2*

"For Christ died for sins ONCE FOR ALL, the RIGHTEOUS for the UNRIGHTEOUS, to bring you to God." *1 Peter 3:18*

"You see, at just the right time, when we were still powerless, Christ died for the UNGODLY...But God demonstrates his own love for us in this: while we were still sinners, CHRIST DIED FOR US." *Romans 5:6 & 8.*

"For the Son of Man came to SEEK and to SAVE what was lost." *Luke 19:10*

"IT IS FINISHED." *John 19:30*

FREE TRACT SOCIETY
P.O. Box 50531 · Los Angeles, CA 90050

# KEEP THESE THOUGHTS BEFORE YOU AND REMEMBER

1. **That you may be saved** - "For God so loved the world that he gave his one and only Son, that whoever believes in him shall not perish but have eternal life." - John 3:16.

2. **That Salvation is free.** -"Come, all you who are thirsty, come to the waters; and you who have no money, come, buy and eat! Come, buy wine and milk without money and without cost." - Isaiah 55:1

3. **That God does not license sin.** -"The soul who sins is the one who will die." - Ezekiel 18:4. "He who does what is sinful is of the devil" - 1 John 3:8

4. **That God is just, and sin must be punished**. - "For the wages of sin is death."- Romans 6:23. "Then death and Hades were thrown into the lake of fire. The lake of fire is the second death. If anyone's name was not found written in the book of life, he was thrown into the lake of fire." Revelation 20:14-15. "The wicked return to the grave, all the nations that forget God." - Psalm 9:17

5. **That God sees your very acts** [whether in thought, word or deed]-you cannot hide them from him, "There is nothing concealed that will not be disclosed, or hidden that will not be made known." - Matthew 10:26

6. **That every Blessing you enjoy in the life, even the air you breathe, comes from God.** Have you thanked Him for them? "Let everything that has breath praise the Lord. Praise the Lord." - Psalm 150:6

7. **That you have been placed here on earth to serve God; and not the devil.**-"'Worship the Lord your God, and serve him only." - Matthew 4:10

8. **That your future life depends upon what you make of the present.** "Do not be deceived: God cannot be mocked. A man reaps what he sows." - Galatians 6:7

# ACCEPT CHRIST NOW!

French audiences to have been Croizette's poison scene – rumoured to have been sensational – in which, by some miracle of stage-craft, she turned a ghastly green in her final moments of agony. But the sensation misfired in England. Whatever interest, aesthetic or otherwise, might have been aroused by Croizette's death scene was briskly dispelled by the actress herself who, most regrettably, fell off her chair whilst taking the poison contained in a ring: a premature demise which curtailed the colourful spectacle of her death-throes and hastily brought down the curtain.

Unfortunate accidents aside, Croizette failed to win the hearts of the British public. Despite the fact that Bernhardt's role in *Le Sphinx* was flimsy and passive in the extreme, she again overshadowed her rival, just as she had done in *L'Etrangère*. Whereas in France audiences and critics had split into two camps – the Croizettists and Bernhardtists – over the issue of artistic superiority, English spectators declared overwhelmingly in favour of Bernhardt. Aware of what appeared to be a growing partisan division among audiences, various of the reviewers, throughout the season, attempted to justify their personal advocacy or antipathy, and what emerged was a debate centred on images of femininity. Reviewing *L'Etrangère*, 'Opera Glass', who was conscious of having described Croizette in less than gracious terms, went on to offer the following explanation or justification of his assessment, by referring to Croizette's conception of the title role in de Musset's *Les Caprices de Marianne*:

> It seems unkind and ungenerous to be perpetually harping upon the inefficiency of Croizette, but those ought to be blamed who have put her in so false a position. She is physically incapable of appearing as an actress of romance or sentiment. Look at her Marianne, for instance, supposed to be the ideal woman of a poet's dreams, the intoxicating influence of a student and a man's soul! Is this the Marianne that anyone can accept? No, she is an actress of modern force, not of poetical abstraction.[30]

The point was pursued by the same reviewer in the following week's edition of the *Era* under the heading 'A High Standard is Essential'. To the earlier comments was now added the ultimate justification of the anti-Croizette lobby: a straightforward lack of acting talent. (Quite simply, she was not a first-rate actress viewed by either English or French standards.) Only the *Pall Mall Gazette* took a pro-Croizette stance in the course of a debate on the histrionic theory of acting.[31] However, the author's avowed preference for the school of self-restraint and dignified understatement – seen as personified in Croizette – was somewhat ironically expressed in the context of a virulent, anti-emotionalist, anti-Bernhardt diatribe.

A large number of reviewers chose to pursue the argument in the *Era* by exploring conflicting ideals of femininity. The debate reached its climax in the now frequently quoted comparison between the two actresses set out in the review of *Hernani* in *The Times*.[32] It was an attempt to explain to the French critic Francisque Sarcey why Bernhardt should have proved so popular with the English public, to the detriment of her fellow actress. Bernhardt's sensitively modulated vocal qualities were favourably compared with the coarser delivery of Croizette, as was the appealingly slender physique of the former with the less graceful, more rotund build of her companion. Moreover, it was the passionate and seductive quality of Bernhardt's interpretation, (providing a sharp contrast to Croizette's relatively restrained manner) which appealed to English audiences. Out of this, Bernhardt had created an image of womanhood which was a paradoxical fusion of individuality and archetypal passion. The actress might assume the mask of Phèdre, Doña Sol or Marguerite, but the woman underneath would possess Bernhardt's own idiosyncratic brand of passion.

For Bernhardt herself, the very concept of femininity was rooted in the art of the theatre, which she retrospectively identified in her treatise on acting as a feminine art.[33] Not only did she argue that it was the one artistic sphere in which women could not only succeed but even outnumber men in their success; she also identified the art of pleasing and externalising inner emotion as essential both to women and to theatre. In to-day's age of articulated feminism, this might appear at first glance to suggest a rather uncomfortable acceptance of conservative ideologies of femininity. Read as a pre- or proto-feminist vocabulary, however, it is clear that Bernhardt is arguing that theatre is a public sphere in which expression of the feminine not only may be voiced and explored, but that it is also intrinsic to the art form. For Bernhardt, the language of theatre is a female language. What she explored was the concept of essential femininity; what it is to be called female. It was no longer simply a question of parading as a desirable love-object, but rather a baring of the female psyche – the inner female life made visible through its language of body, face and voice. Where theatre is defined as the sphere of making the invisible visible, so woman is closer to the invisible than the male.

This was facetiously recognised by several reviewers in their commentaries on the female reaction to Bernhardt's London performances. Matthew Arnold, pondering in retrospect the infatuation of the English public with the French actress, referred to the number of 'great ladies who by the acting of Mdlle. Sarah Bernhardt were revealed to themselves, and who could not resist the desire of telling her so'.[34] That in the majority of cases female soul-searching still stopped short at the external trappings of femininity cannot be denied. One has only to look at the numerous fashion columns for the 'lady spectator', accompanying reviews, to see that this is so.

For a particular group of women, however, Bernhardt's performances provided a renewed interest in the theatre as well as a female interest. It was noted that Bernhardt's classical performances attracted a large group of erudite young ladies, and on such occasions, the boxes usually filled by 'representatives of careless frivolity' instead contained 'young and spectacled ladies who all appear to be related to headmasters or to be distantly connected with college tutors.'[35] It was consequently suggested that 'if this goes on it may be a good speculation to start an excursion train between Oxford and Cambridge on these classical nights for the sake of these higher educated women and the undergraduates of Girton'.[36] Certainly at a classical Saturday matinée, more than half the audience would be female. Whether breathing new life into the classics for the 'bluestockings' or appealing to the 'souls' of fashionable ladies who could afford to luxuriate in spectacles of female anguish or martyrdom, the enormity of her appeal was unquestionable and inevitably, as the season wore on, provoked criticism.

Already, prior to the company's departure for London, the issue of private performances had proved inflamatory. It remained so as Bernhardt went ahead with her dramatic sketches during the season, performed in several fashionable drawing rooms. To the tune of one hundred guineas, London salons were treated to the second act of *Phèdre*, with her Odéon success, *Le Passant*, or a specially written piece, *Le Pari d'une grande dame*. The latter, a duologue, simply gave Bernhardt the opportunity to play Bernhardt.

It depicts an actress who has supposedly achieved success through the notoriety surrounding her artistic endeavours, notably her sculpture. The wager of the *grande dame* is to expose the actress's claim to genius. The lady calls on the actress in her studio, whereupon the latter seizes the opportunity to model a bust of the visitor, and the lady leaves, highly delighted and now convinced of the actress's genius. It was a highly theatrical piece and, as such, simply mirrored the controversy surrounding the Bernhardt talent-versus-publicity debate.

Tension over the private performances increased when Bernhardt missed a public afternoon performance of *L'Etrangère*, on Saturday, 21 June. Indignation at the last-minute cancellation, as an embarrassed Coquelin was left to explain the actress's indisposition to a disappointed audience (which included members of royalty), was aggravated by the knowledge that Bernhardt had been giving a private performance in Belgrave Square the previous night. A letter from 'Belgravia' to the editor of *The Times* on 24 June raised the question of whether the audience for the following Saturday, 28 June, could expect similar treatment. Bernhardt, wounded by the suggestion, replied on 26 June with a declaration of respect for the English public and an explanation of her illness, her vomiting of blood, which had persisted throughout the Saturday morning in question. Clearly, there is every indication that Bernhardt was overtaxing her strength with her acting schedule, private performances and public functions, though she took care not to disappoint her audiences again. That she should chose to overcommit herself is symptomatic both of a financial need and a desire to establish future contacts and friendships within the ranks of English royalty and among well-to-do aristocratic circles.

Among her other public activities, Sarah's exhibition of sculpture and paintings and her involvement in the French Fête brought her more limelight. In an *atelier* in Piccadilly, Bernhardt held her one-woman exhibition consisting of sixteen oil-paintings and nine sculptured pieces. One painting in particular, *Retour de l'Eglise*, depicting a young lady dressed in black for Palm Sunday, attracted a good deal of attention and, according to Bernhardt's *Mémoires*, was purchased by Prince Leopold.[37] Of the sculptured pieces, it was the group, *Après la tempête*, representing a drowned fisher-boy on the knees of his distraught mother, which was considered the finest exhibit. Overall it was agreed that, although by no means technically proficient, Sarah's art showed much promise, and the paintings in particular were noted for their use of colour. In any event, the exhibition attracted crowds of dignitaries from the world of the arts, politics (Gladstone), royalty (the Prince and Princess of Wales) and high society. Not least amongst these was Sarah herself:

> A plain black jacket and skirt, a tumbled leghorn hat and a black velvet trimming, a wisp of muslin about her neck, a bouquet of real roses clinging to her dress – and there was Sarah Bernhardt. There was no attempt at decoration or display. She was the one simply dressed woman in the assembly, but she carried with her the famous stick, a plain little malacca cane, very short and very simple, and she delighted everybody.[38]

At the French Fête, organised to raise funds for the London French Hospital, it was again Sarah who took the leading role. At this charitable occasion which took place on 7–8 July, Sarah's stall, which was furnished by Howell and Jones and stocked with a plethora of Bernhardt memorabilia such as plaques, plates, photographs and portrait copies, became the focus of much attention. Capitalising on her celebrity, Bernhardt could name her price and on the first day of the fête raised a record sum of £256.

It was precisely this link between art and commerce that augmented the censorious tone, which had been gradually creeping into the reviews of her critics. Ironically, the most vocal condemnation came not from the English press, but in the form of angry tirades unleashed from the French capital. From the French point of view, Bernhardt appeared to be selling out to stardom and betraying the tradition and honour of the company to which she belonged. Spearheaded by Albert Wolff in *Le Figaro* (27 June), speculations and pure inventions – talk, for example, of her fencing in the garden, smoking cigars or dressing in male attire – came thick and fast. In reply to Wolff's attack, Sarah sent a telegram, stating her intention to resign. A flood of reassurances and dissuasions from her Comédie colleagues were immediately forthcoming. Likewise, John Hollingshead printed reassurances in *The Times* on 1 July for the Gaiety audiences, stating that the Gaiety season would not be affected in any way. Though Sarah's definitive rupture with the Comédie did not come until after the return to France, it was indisputably clear that her star-personality was becoming too large, too individual and too rebellious for the national theatre to handle.

Sarah duly completed her Gaiety season as she had begun it – playing to packed houses. At the end of her appearances, the English critics resumed their discussion of the relative claims of talent and notoriety in accounting for Sarah's success. American novelist and critic, Henry James, followed the puritanical line taken by the French press and lamented the Bernhardt 'vogue' as 'the success of a celebrity pure and simple'.[39] Clement Scott's *Theatre*, on the other hand, described it as inevitable that 'excess' should provoke 'excess' and thus that 'extravagant censure' should follow 'gushing enthusiasm'.[40] A second article in the same issue went on to vindicate Bernhardt's private performances on the grounds that, although she was the greatest attraction of the Comédie, her remuneration was meagre, and in consequence she had every right to explore other avenues of income. The sum total she received for her public performances in London is quoted as £150, whereas (it was pointed out) 'any American or continental manager would engage her for at least three months at £100 a night'.[41]

If the French critics had shown themselves to be jealous and suspicious of Bernhardt's stardom, the attitude that emerged from the English critics was rather envy of a nation which could boast a thriving repertory of modern drama, as well as a national theatre and school of dramatic art. One of the most passionate pleas for an English national theatre on the French model came from Matthew Arnold, who ventured the view that whatever else the Gaiety season had accomplished, it had certainly reopened

English eyes to the 'irresistibility' of theatre. Though Arnold saw Bernhardt as 'wanting in high intellectual power', he nevertheless acknowledged her as the potent catalyst behind a resurgence of interest in the dramatic arts on the part of the English public:

> And still, even now that they are gone, when I pass along the Strand and come opposite to the Gaiety Theatre, I see a fugitive vision of delicate features under a shower of hair and a cloud of lace, and hear the voice of Mdlle. Sarah Bernhardt saying in its most caressing tones to the Londoners: 'The theatre is irresistible; *organise the theatre!*'[42]

That Arnold should, almost inadvertently, detect a link between irresistible femininity and the art of the theatre is neither surprising nor fortuitous, for the delicate features of the actress seemed to mirror the essence of the medium itself. And future London seasons would provide further testimony to the irresistibility of Sarah's art.

# Notes

1. Sarah Bernhardt, *L'Art du théâtre*, p. 150.
2. Ibid.
3. *Era*, 8 June 1879.
4. *Daily Telegraph*, 16 June 1879.
5. Sarah Bernhardt, *L'Art du théâtre*, pp. 133–4.
6. Ibid., p. 135.
7. *The Times*, 3 June 1879.
8. *Era*, 8 June 1879.
9. *Daily News*, 3 June 1879.
10. *Pall Mall Gazette*, 10 July 1879.
11. *The Times*, 27 June 1879.
12. *Era*, 29 June 1879.
13. *Morning Post*, 30 June 1879.
14. Joseph Knight, *Theatrical Notes* (London: Lawrence & Bullen, 1893), p. 269.
15. *Morning Post*, 18 June 1879.
16. *The Times*, 18 June 1879.
17. *Spectator*, 14 June 1879.
18. *The Times*, 11 June 1879.
19. Ibid.

20. *Morning Post*, 10 June 1879.
21. *Spectator*, 14 June 1879.
22. Gerda Taranow, *The Art Within the Legend* (Princeton: Princeton University Press, 1972), Chapter 5, 'Paradox'.
23. *Era*, 15 June 1879.
24. *Morning Post*, 1 July 1879.
25. Ibid.
26. *Daily Telegraph*, 5 June 1879.
27. *Morning Post*, 4 June 1879.
28. *Spectator*, 7 June 1879.
29. *Daily Telegraph*, 5 June 1879.
30. *Era*, 8 June 1879.
31. *Pall Mall Gazette*, 10 July 1879.
32. *The Times*, 11 June 1879.
33. Sarah Bernhardt, *L'Art du théâtre*, p. 145.
34. Matthew Arnold, *The Complete Prose Works*, ed. R. H. Super, 11 vols (Ann Arbor: University of Michigan Press, 1973), vol. IX, p. 65.
35. *Era*, 22 June 1879.
36. Ibid.
37. Sarah Bernhardt, *Mémoires*, vol. II, p. 116.
38. *Era*, 22 June 1879.
39. Henry James, *The Scenic Art* (London: Rupert Hart Davis, 1949), p. 128.
40. *Theatre*, 1 Aug. 1879, p. 1.
41. Ibid., p. 4.
42. Matthew Arnold, *The Complete Prose Works*, vol. IX, p. 85.

# 3 Women in Love: 'Sarah aux Camélias'

After the return of the Comédie Française to Paris (conducted in a very quiet manner), Sarah's position was particularly uncomfortable. Given that the Paris press had made the most of her absence to stir up hostility and to further the idea that she sought only to promote herself, to the detriment of the rest of the company, Sarah fully expected a fight. Anonymous and vitriolic letters warning her to stay away from the opening ceremony, which had been planned to mark the company's return, had already reached her. However, given her independent and determined nature, Sarah was neither to be intimidated nor to be persuaded by an anxious Perrin to stay away. These threats merely served to arouse Sarah's fighting spirit, and when, on the night of the ceremony, the company paired off to pay homage to Molière and to present themselves to the Parisian public, Sarah broke with tradition and went forward alone to the footlights, fully anticipating a hostile confrontation with her audience. Instead, her independent, angry and defiant gesture earned a burst of thunderous applause from the audience. The French press, on the other hand, remained hostile towards her, and it was now abundantly clear that Sarah's days with the Comédie were indeed numbered.

The pretext for the long-overdue rupture came with Perrin's plans for the production of Emile Augier's mid-century drama, *L'Aventurière*. For Sarah, who intensely disliked the part of the antipathetic adventuress Clorinde, this was the last straw. She was not only disenchanted with the role, but she had also had insufficient time to study it. She probably also knew how unpopular the role had proved in past performances: the unsympathetic nature of the part seemingly rubbed off on the actresses who played it, as Mlle Anaïs, the original Clorinde, and Mme Plessy, who had subsequently played the part in April 1860, had discovered. (In England the play had enjoyed more success in the guise of Tom Robertson's adaptation *Home*, but this was because, as the new title implied, the dramatic emphasis had switched from the adventuress – now re-conceived as a 'merry widow' – to the family.)

Sarah pleaded with Perrin to consider postponing the opening, but her entreaties were ignored. Inevitably, Bernhardt played the part very badly, and the press united in a deluge of disparaging criticism. Consequently, after only one performance, given on 17 April 1880, Sarah broke with the Comédie, beating a hasty retreat to Le Havre and leaving Croizette to take over the role. A lawsuit, instigated by the Comédie, was set in motion almost immediately. Sarah never had a chance of winning, and it was a battle which cost her one-hundred-thousand francs in damages, plus the loss of forty-three-thousand francs held in the pension fund. In compensation, she found a more lucrative income than she could ever have earned at the Comédie, under the aegis of the impresario Jarrett, who had for some time been pressing for an American contract and whose proposals were now accepted. Meanwhile, Sarah returned to London for a second Gaiety season, for which she had signed with Hollingshead and Mayer.

Though Sarah no longer had the backing of the illustrious Comédie players, she could still draw on a number of talented artists who had chosen to throw in their lot with her. For supporting female roles she had the talents of Mme Devoyod (formerly with the Comédie), Mary Kalb, Mary Jullien, and her own half-sister Jeanne, who had adopted the famous surname of Bernhardt. Her actors included the talented Pierre Berton, Talbot (also ex-Comédie), and Train and Dieudonné from the Vaudeville. The celebrated Coquelin was to have appeared with Sarah for the second half of the season in June, but Perrin found a loophole to keep him in Paris and prevent him from fulfilling his engagement.

Now that Bernhardt's beloved Paris had expressed an eagerness to witness the assumed decline of her career, it was to her London audience that Sarah chose to offer her new creations. Setting up on her own was clearly a bold move, but Sarah had undoubtedly weighed up the risks of finding Paris closed to her talents. Her will to succeed, both artistically and financially, made such a move inevitable. She had recognised that despite the

Comédie's accusations to the contrary, she was its greatest box-office draw and that greater rewards could be found on an international than a national stage. Moveover, she was freed from the constraints of Perrin's often ill-chosen roles and was able to perform show-case parts which displayed her emotional style at its best, a strategy which suited both the star and her financial backers.

Sarah opened her London season in the title role of Scribe and Legouvé's *Adrienne Lecouvreur*, which had originally been created by Rachel. Based on the life of the eighteenth-century actress, the part ranges from breathless scenes of amorous rivalry, through formal recitations of a set-piece from *Phèdre* and of La Fontaine's *Les deux pigeons*, to the quasi-obligatory scene of agonising death. In view of its challenging scope, the role had attracted several interpreters in the aftermath of Rachel, notably Mme Ristori, Mme Favart, the Polish-born actress Mme Modjeska, and Bernhardt's rival of the Odéon years, Adèle Page; each had brought a different approach to the part. The panther-like power of Rachel's reading (in 1849) was replaced by Ristori's reserved, classical conception and the 'splendid severity' of Mme Favart.[1] Bernhardt's interpretation marked a further departure from that of her predecessors.

Adrienne does not make her appearance until act two, where she is seen in the foyer of the Comédie Française, preparing for her role as Roxane in Racine's *Bajazet* and encountering her lover Maurice. From the moment of her first entrance, Bernhardt established and highlighted the image of amorous womanhood which had been the hallmark of her roles the previous year:

This act gives to the actress scope for that unrestrained display of feminine tenderness in which lies the supreme strength of Mdlle. Sarah Bernhardt. It would be difficult to imagine anything more caressing and *caline*, more fond and playful, more subtly reductive than the acting of Sarah Bernhardt in these scenes with Maurice, or more plaintively musical than her recital of the tender verses of La Fontaine. All the most irresistible weapons in Mdlle. Bernhardt's armoury of fascination can be here brought into play – the wooing music of her sweet and silvery voice, the winning winding caresses of her lithe arms and slender figure, all the vocabulary of a loving woman's self-surrendering *abandon* in look, voice, and action.[2]

This picture of an irresistible seductress was offered as an alternative to Rachel's tigerish passion, and those who had anticipated, predicted or indeed actually wished for Sarah to fail were disappointed. By the end of act two, the actress had won back an audience which – in contrast to the enthusiasm of 1879 – had begun watching in a silence which was somewhat distant and reserved.

The climax of the drama comes in the fourth act, as Adrienne recognises the vindictive Princesse de Bouillon (Mme Devoyod) as her rival for the affection of Maurice de Saxe and comes to believe that she has been betrayed in love. The recitation from *Phèdre* given in the princess's drawing room provides Adrienne with the opportunity to denounce her rival. In Rachel's interpretation, this had been the supreme moment of her show of formidable passion, which had mesmerised her audiences earlier in the century. But whereas Rachel's Adrienne grew more terrible and awesome in the grip of passion, Bernhardt played the scene without abandoning her image of fragile restraint, though now taxed to breaking-point by the inner pressure of intense emotion:

> She grows to a white heat of passion as she crosses swords with her rival; it is the concentration of nervous power seen in the quivering lip and tightened hand. The whole frame, thin and wasted as it is, seems to shake under the repression needed to tame the demon that is arising in this frail and disappointed creature. The revenge comes in the 'Phèdre' recital that closes with that sharp hysterical scream so natural under the circumstances, and so appropriate to the physical condition of the nervous woman who has been hitherto portrayed.[3]

Opinion, however, was divided as to how successful this was as a representation of irrupting fury. Rachel had vented her rage before the princess without moving towards her, but Bernhardt's method was to 'advance across the stage towards her detested rival and hurl the outrage in the words of "Phèdre" into her very face, with outstretched finger almost touching her'. This was considered by at least one reviewer to be 'overstrained' and – as behaviour appropriate to the drawing-room of a princess – 'extravagant' and 'improbable'.[4]

For those who felt that the passages of defiance were the least successful elements in Sarah's interpretation, the pathos which she brought to the death scene more than compensated for the arguably strained effects of the previous tableaux. Here, in place of the prolonged and agonised writhings of Rachel, emotion was expressed mainly by vocal means, in the harrowing tones of a woman who protests she is too young to die. Though reconciled with her lover at the last, the poisoned bouquet deposited by the vengeful princess has worked its fatal effect. Adrienne's dying moments were characterised by Sarah's broken cries of despair – her fingers tearing through dishevelled hair, and her arms outstretched in supplication – as she beseeched delivery from the cruel destiny which had overtaken her. Sarah's performance once more transported the audience to a shared plane of suffering which had to be endured in silence, until it could finally be relieved in the tumultuous applause which followed the curtain.

In the first week of her second season Bernhardt also revived her *Phèdre*, with M. Train replacing Mounet-Sully in the role of Hippolyte. 'As before', wrote the *Daily Telegraph* reviewer, 'the despairing scenes were the best, the introspection far more effective than the declamation, and when the actress beat her breast or bowed her head, tore her hair or writhed in very agony, the art was Grecian in its tendency and eminently picturesque.'[5] Discussions of Bernhardt's suitability for the respective parts of Adrienne Lecouvreur and Phèdre inevitably emerged during the week she appeared in both parts. The *Pall Mall Gazette*, which had been so uncomplimentary the previous year, showed signs of a less prejudiced and more analytical approach in its comparative assessment of her work. The reviewer considered that Adrienne was a role far more suited to Bernhardt's skills than that of Racine's heroine, because the part was 'modern' in conception, as was 'the cast of her imagination and temper'.[6] Though not openly stated, the basis of this judgement probably lay in an objection to the inclusion of pantomimic gesture in Racinian tragedy, for the purists considered Bernhardt's 'modern' excesses quite acceptable in a play such as *Adrienne Lecouvreur* but inappropriate to classical drama, which traditionally required the statuesque and quiet dignity of a Rachel. Bernhardt's gestures were a far cry from dignified restraint; in tableaux of womanly anguish, she reversed corporeal reserve into agitated tremors, shuddering and shaking through every limb, so that her long thin arms quivered

41

from the shoulder to the very fingertips of her delicate hands. Conversely, there were some who welcomed the break with tradition and regarded, for example, the way in which the hands of her Phèdre, 'hungering for unblest caresses,' tore at the unloved body as a signification of 'thorough humanness' and a 'revelation' in artistic method.[7]

In addition to playing Adrienne and Phèdre in her first week, Bernhardt also appeared as Edouard V, in Casimir Delavigne's *Les Enfants d'Edouard*, which had been premiered at the Théâtre Français in 1833. This play, based on the controversial facts surrounding the murder of the two princes in the Tower of London, is a rather unsatisfactory verse–drama, uneasily poised between Classical and Romantic influences. The main role was generally considered to be that of Edouard's brother, the Duke of York, but Sarah entrusted this part (a portrait of boyish mischief and high spirits) to her sister Jeanne. As the more delicate and reserved brother, Bernhardt pursued the picturesque, graceful and lyrical tableau of boyhood which she had initiated during the Odéon years in her *travesti* role of Zanetto in *Le Passant*:

> What is chiefly noticeable is the unstained purity and delicacy of the presentation. Looking, in her sombre purple garb, the ideal of graceful boyhood, and assuming, as it seems by instinct, poses every one of which is a model of refinement and beauty. Madlle. Bernhardt gives the entire performance the value of a supremely touching and tender poem.[8]

Reviews of this production were few, as critical interest tended to focus on Bernhardt's Adrienne. The *Pall Mall Gazette* was an exception: it concluded its comparative analysis of the week's offerings with an appraisal of her Edouard V, which, of the three roles under scrutiny, the reviewer judged to be her finest creation.[9] The appeal for this critic was largely a consequence of the emotionally uncomplicated nature of the part, which effectively deprived Sarah of any scope for what he perceived to be her worst excesses of vocal delivery and gesticulation; indeed, he could have wished that the grace and decorum with which she played her *travesti* role were equally characteristic of her classical heroines.

Just as *Adrienne Lecouvreur* had been the main attraction of the first week, *Froufrou*, which opened on Monday 31 May, was the centre of interest in the second. If the shadow of Rachel had haunted her Adrienne, Bernhardt's appearance in this next play would inevitably summon up the ghost of Aimée Desclée, who had played the title role in the original production at the Gymnase in October 1869. The joint authors of the piece, Meilhac and Halévy, had conceived the part of Gilberte (known as Froufrou) especially for Desclée, who had given an outstanding and memorable performance as the empty-headed *parisienne*. Froufrou, as the familiar name implies, is a frivolous and pleasure-loving young woman whose lack of sound judgement leads her into an unfortunate alliance, which has been encouraged by her more down-to-earth sister Louise. This marriage is plunged into crisis when Gilberte misconstrues her sister's solicitous interest in the *ménage* as an attempt to usurp the affections of her son and husband. Impulsively, Gilberte forsakes her home for an unhappy love-nest and only returns to the bosom of her family to beg forgiveness of her husband and to die before his eyes, after he has fought a duel with her lover. Although the role had been designed as a showcase for the unique talents of Desclée, its unrestrained emotionality might have been tailor-made for Bernhardt, and as some reviewers rightly foresaw, it would become one of the mainstays of her repertoire.

It was generally felt that, in the first two acts, Bernhardt did not quite capture the note of unthinking superficiality demanded by the role. The essence of the part required the actress to project a sense of innocent, child-like irresponsibility, devoid – initially, at least – of any sense of guilt or scruples of conscience; this was precisely where Aimée Desclée had excelled. Bernard Henry Becker put his finger on the problem in the *Theatre*, when he cited the absence of 'light-hearted unconsciousness' as the underlying flaw in Sarah's interpretation: it created the impression rather of the 'obstinacy of a woman with a purpose' than 'the petulant wilfulness of a spoiled child'. In other respects, however, he described the performance as 'most carefully-studied and beautiful'.[10] In the third and fourth acts – as the growing anxiety of a troubled woman replaces erstwhile frivolity – Bernhardt's portrayal gained in conviction and refinement. Her parting line as she declares to her sister, 'Je m'avoue vaincue . . . je te cède la place,' held the audiences spellbound. The build-up to this departure bore all the traits of anguish which had come to be identified with the Bernhardt heroine. The bold physical gestures employed to convey deep inner anxiety together with the resourceful and inventive use of stage-space bore cogent witness to her consumate grasp of dramatic technique, and for once, there were no objections to this vividly gesticulatory mode of performance, which was considered entirely appropriate to the role in question:

> In the manner in which the fingers during her interview with her husband and her sister, in which her future destiny is decided, catch now at the borders of the couch on which she sits, now at the leaves of the book beneath her hand, and in the manner in which she rolls her handkerchief into a ball and then tears it into strips, with which in her fervid and uncertain walk she strews the carpet, the kind of nervous rage, which is all that Frou Frou is capable of feeling, is superbly shown.[11]

As Gilberte's mounting desperation reached new heights in the fourth act, so too did Bernhardt's histrionic display. In order to dissuade her husband from duelling, Bernhardt's Gilberte positively clung and tore at his body in her efforts to avert the impending duel. The spectacle of her frenzied entreaties was rapidly followed by the starkly contrasting death scene, a tableau of the most tender and pathetic beauty.

For this role Bernhardt assumed no less than seven changes of wardrobe, the successive switches from riding attire to evening dress, morning and day wear, culminating in a penitential, black gown. Thus clad she knelt at the feet of her husband to implore his pardon and request that she be buried in a simple, white dress, offset by a motif of delicate roses in order to re-create, at the last, the image of the old Froufrou. This cameo of kneeling supplication caught the attention of several reviewers who noted the poignant way in which the posture accentuated the remorseful plea. The gesture was to become a stock-in-trade for many of Bernhardt's distressed heroines.

A season that had begun with some trepidation, therefore, ended in a triumph. Even those publications which had adopted an anti-Bernhardt stance the previous year – in particular, the

*Spectator* and the *Pall Mall Gazette* – while they still had some reservations, were beginning to show a more positive attitude towards the actress. The other members of her company received scant attention from the press, even though she had been very ably seconded in *Froufrou* by M. Train, who took the role of the husband Sartorys – he had actually been cast as the lover Valréas in the original production – and Pierre Berton who gave a creditable account of the far from sympathetic role of the rival.

Although Coquelin's failure to appear in London was regrettable, it did not prove disastrous. As a fairly light-weight complement to her two resounding successes – as Adrienne Lecouvreur and Froufrou, roles which she continued to portray throughout the season – Bernhardt now introduced the slight but effective verse-drama *Jean-Marie* which had featured in the Odéon repertoire. The English public made its acquaintance in June, on a double bill with Molière's *L'Avare* which starred Berton. It was to provide the pretext for a display of passionate acting. Set on the coast of Brittany, the single act depicts the unexpected return of the heroine's childhood sweetheart Jean-Marie, who has been presumed lost at sea for several years. Having given him up for dead, the long-suffering Thérèse has taken an older husband and must now conceal her passion for the young sailor and banish him from her presence. As the curtain rose, Thérèse (played by Bernhardt) appeared as a languorous and graceful figure in her humble cottage dwelling. But the return of Jean-Marie marked a change of mood, as it signalled the re-kindling of their former passion and a struggle for the heroine, momentarily tempted to succumb to his entreaties:

> For a moment she rests passive and subject, but the thought of her husband, his wrecked life, and his dishonoured home flashes upon her. Now she is strong, she tears herself from him, urges him with eager impetuous words to quit her, shuts her ears to his last appeal, hears him go, and then with statuesque despair turns to face the blank monotonous despair of future life.[12]

The whole play lasted little more than thirty minutes, but it was replete with pathos and tender emotion.

For a virtuoso performer there were certain advantages to be gained from the practice, currently in vogue, of devising programmes consisting of short plays or single acts extracted from full-length dramas. Sarah Bernhardt was partial to such 'anthologies' and was careful to choose selections which would display the spectrum of her particular strengths and skills in the most impressive light. For her benefit night in the Gaiety season (16 June 1880) she assembled a programme consisting of *Jean-Marie*, the fourth act of *Rome vaincue* and the final act of *Hernani*. As the *Era* described, the juxtaposition of such dissimilar roles as that of the young Thérèse (in *Jean-Marie*) and the old, blind Roman matron Posthumia (in *Rome vaincue*) afforded an excellent gauge of the actress's versatility.[13] Though the distressed mother-figure of Posthumia was as far removed from Thérèse as the Doña Sol which followed it, all three parts offered the common revelation of female figure *in extremis*. A minority view of critics did, in fact, suggest that these three interpretations were virtually interchangeable and that this was the case with all Bernhardt's creations,[14] but the generality conceded that the programme had highlighted the range and adaptability of the actress.

This second London season came to an end on Saturday, 19 June with a programme of excerpts from *Adrienne Lecouvreur*, *Rome vaincue* and *Froufrou*. With this tour Bernhardt had not simply consolidated the success of the last London engagements: she had begun to win over her former detractors. Those who had shown themselves highly critical of the previous season were becoming more receptive to her talents and busied themselves with further analyses of her acting style, which the latest appearances had exposed to closer reflection and scrutiny. Furthermore, her English successes had effectively ended any notion of a failed career. Even though the French critics had been generally hostile, representatives from the Paris press had, nevertheless, attended the London season. Sarcey, Vitu and Lapommeraye all witnessed her performance as Adrienne and, however grudgingly at first, had come around to an acknowledgement of her real talents and her deserving success with the public. They even expressed regret that she should have left the Comédie. That Perrin also lamented the loss of his box-office draw was evident when he sent M. Got as an emissary of the Comédie to solicit Sarah's return.[15] The idea of rejoining the company was out of the question; the London triumph was proof positive that Sarah could succeed in her career as an independent woman. She now had a far greater earning capacity, was free to choose her own repertoire and company, and was no longer cramped by the rules and regulations of a tradition-bound theatre.

Dismissing Perrin's proposal, Sarah toured her two major London successes in Brussels and Copenhagen and in September gave performances of the same plays in France (the itinerary was arranged by her old friend of the Odéon days Félix Duquesnel), before setting sail to conquer the American public in October. The American tour (fortunately for Sarah) was to prove highly lucrative and showed that the American public, like the English, were enthusiastic about the new international star and prepared to cope with a foreign repertoire of drama and its French delivery. Sarah quotes the total receipts from productions as 2,667,600 francs; an average of 17,100 francs per performance.[16] In the main, her repertoire consisted of tried and tested favourites: *Adrienne Lecouvreur*, *Froufrou*, *Hernani*, *L'Etrangère*, *Phèdre* and *Le Sphinx*. (Of these, *Froufrou* was the most frequently performed, receiving 41 performances out of a total of 156 performances). There were also two new plays in the repertoire, both by Dumas *fils*: *La Princesse Georges*, in which Sarah took the role of the Princesse de Birac (again premièred by Aimée Desclée) and *La Dame aux Camélias*, in which Sarah took the role of Marguerite Gautier, which had been created by Marie Doche. Whereas *La Princesse Georges* was played on only three occasions, *La Dame aux Camélias* proved easily the most popular play in her repertoire and was given 65 performances during the tour. It was this piece which Sarah chose to inaugurate her next London season, her third consecutive year on the English stage; it was greeted by a blaze of acclaim.

Premiered on 11 June 1881, Bernhardt's interpretation of Marguerite was the first opportunity an English audience had had of seeing Dumas's original play. Hitherto it had been suppressed on moral grounds by the Lord Chamberlain, although it was evidently acceptable in the guise of Verdi's *La Traviata* and the emasculated adaptation *Heartsease* by James Mortimer, in which Mme Modjeska had scored a success the previous year. Dumas's play was an early attempt to dramatise

47

the realities of the courtesan world and to present Marguerite as a Magdalen-figure, worthy of redemption. From this point of view, it was considered daring by many; for others (including the censor) it was simply immoral. The Prince of Wales, who attended the première with the Princess, is frequently cited as having been instrumental in obtaining the licence for the production. As, however, the performance was given in French, as was always the case in Sarah's productions, the language barrier, in this instance, helped to create an acceptable and comfortable moral distance between the characters represented and the puritanical English public.

The courtesan world of the pre-Franco-Prussian War era was something which Bernhardt had experienced at first hand – had, indeed, grown up in. She could, therefore, combine her seductive artistry with intimate knowledge to give an astonishing performance in a role which was to become arguably the most popular and successful of her career. In future, whenever funds were low or her repertoire suffered from a dearth of new material, *La Dame aux Camélias* could be relied upon to fill the theatre. For the 'connoisseurs', wrote the biographer Louis Verneuil (Sarah's grandson-in-law), her most popular role was Phèdre, but for the 'crowd' it was unquestionably her Marguerite.[17]

The success of the play depended upon the actress's ability to transform Marguerite into a pure and angelic being on a spiritual plane far removed from her courtesan existence. Sarah succeeded in investing her Marguerite with such an 'ineffable sweetness', that the reviewer for *The Times* suggested one might almost 'see the halo of a saint upon her forehead'.[18] The confrontation scene between Marguerite and Armand's father, M. Duval, was universally acclaimed as an instance of artistic excellence:

> In the scene in which she learns from the father of her lover how inadequate has been the brief penitence she has rashly thought enough for her redemption and stands face to face with the implacable destinies, the surging emotions which beset her, and their slow subjugation by the resolution of self-sacrifice, were manifested in triumphant fashion. It was, moreover, no heroine by whom the conquest was won, but a shrinking, nervous, impressionable woman, who knew her own weakness and fled while strength was left her from appeals she felt herself powerless to resist.[19]

After M. Duval's departure, Bernhardt gave another supreme demonstration of a woman in torment. Marguerite's inner turmoil and agitation were made manifest in half-uttered cries, a body which struggled to contain the grief which seeped through to 'the thin fingers', 'clutching' almost 'piercing' the fabric of her dress.[20]

For the death scene she introduced the novel technique of standing until the last breath of life and then falling forward onto the chest of Armand (played by M. Angelo). For those more familiar with Marie Doche's gradual and graceful decline on a couch, while clasping the hand of her lover, this was considered rather stagey and artificial. Others, including Sarcey (again present for Bernhardt's latest creation), saw it as a gesture of defiance.[21] Like Adrienne, Marguerite desires to live and to love – to survive despite the gods (in this instance, the custodians of bourgeois morality).

A close examination of a cross-section of reviews reveals the ways in which the English critics saw Bernhardt's talents developing in this third season. Earlier charges that all Bernhardt's roles were virtually interchangeable, and even bordered on self-parody, now gave way to an acknowledgement of her ability to achieve total absorption in the diverse character-types she portrayed:

> When, going out of her own nature, an actress enters within the body, so to speak, of an imaginary conception which she animates and informs, when there is not an intonation of voice or a movement of limb that is not characteristic of the adopted individuality, and when every conceivable phase of character is presented with absolute identification, it is surely permissible to say that, so far as regards the opportunities presented, greater acting has not been and will not be.[22]

The *Pall Mall Gazette*, which in the second season had moved towards a more cordial assessment and a more rigorous, less prejudiced analysis of Bernhardt's acting technique than it had offered during her first tour, embarked on a considered reappraisal of her art.[23] While continuing to balk at some persistent mannerisms which he still found excessive and histrionic – notably the habit of reacting to threats of rejection by her lover with dramatic falls and similar gymnastics in death scenes – the reviewer could not otherwise fault the performance. In her portrayals

of Romantic *grande passion* Sarah was now regarded as un-
surpassed. The abandoned behaviour which had always been the
dominant trait of Bernhardt's love-stricken heroines, but which
had sometimes seemed exaggerated, was completely suited to
the role of Marguerite. In truth, the passion of Bernhardt's
women knew no bounds: they caressed their lovers in moments of
(usually all too brief) ecstasy and clutched them feverishly
whenever disaster threatened. Her representations of love were
entirely modern in conception, startlingly new in terms of their
seductive and sexual undercurrents (judged more appropriate for
Marguerite, the 'whore with a heart of gold' in the *demi-monde*,
than for the distressed Phèdre in the world of classical tragedy).

As an instrument of passionate utterance her voice, too, had
gained in effect. The *Pall Mall Gazette*, reviewing *Adrienne Lecouvreur* and *Froufrou* the previous year, had already drawn attention
to Bernhardt's highly idiosyncratic vocal delivery.[24] Briefly, she
would sacrifice the emphasis of the individual word to the articulation and cadence of longer passages. Where, on the one hand, it
was argued that this method was detrimental to bringing out the
full meaning of the text, there was no denying that, in moments of
acute emotion, her intonation and characteristically rapid delivery could prove highly effective. This had been true of the later
scenes in *Froufrou*, and it proved even more appropriate in *La
Dame aux Camélias*, where the rapid enunciation of lines caught to
perfection the accents of heartfelt amorous declaration:

> There is an indefinable quality in the voice of this actress which
> renders her able at all times to hold powerful sway over the feelings of
> the spectators in scenes of this touching character; but her highly
> finished art is after all shown more in the variety of expression which
> she brings to bear upon a part which might easily become tame and
> monotonous; for this is not a play distinguished by clever surprises or
> by ingenuity of intrigue.[25]

In all of this there was an elusive magic which reviewers failed –
and acknowledged they failed – to capture in their analytical
vocabularies. The extraordinary spell could only be hinted at.
The *Pall Mall Gazette* fell back on the conventional analogy with
music and its direct appeal to the emotions.[26] Though audiences
often seemed distant or aloof at the beginning of a performance,

they would gradually be drawn by Bernhardt's peculiar magnetism; the actress melted their resistance and eventually had them crying into their handkerchiefs, as the tears fell from her own eyes. (It was calculated that even more tears were shed in the final moments of her Marguerite, than on the death of Froufrou!)

One reliable indicator of fame or notoriety comes when a personality is considered sufficiently well-known and identifiable to be a subject for caricature. During Sarah's fortnight of performances in *La Dame aux Camélias* and *Froufrou* (the only plays produced in the season of 1881), Mr William Henry Rice presented in St James's Hall his impersonation of 'Sarah Heartburn'. The caricature had been a big hit in Philadelphia, but in London it was considered a disappointing spoof: Bernhardt's mannerisms were scarcely recognisable, and the comedy, such as it was, resulted rather from the weak and farcical dramatic situations portrayed.[27] A parody of Bernhardt's death scenes, for which Mr Rice created a ghastly half-white and half-black face with the help of smeared charcoal, showed, if nothing else, the extent to which such tableaux had become prominent and characteristic features of her roles. Around this time, too, *Froufrou* became the butt of parody in the short comedy, *Seeing FrouFrou*, which was presented at the Globe Theatre. (Mme Modjeska was, in fact, also playing the unfortunate Gilberte in her season at the Princess's Theatre, so the combined efforts of the two acting celebrities had evidently exposed the play sufficiently to make it a target for the satirists.)

Sarah's 1881 season was limited to two weeks. She then toured her productions around major English provinces, while London audiences were entertained by some of the other European performers or companies who brought a cosmopolitan flavour to the capital's stages during the summer months, when resident companies took their annual break or likewise embarked on provincial tours. Paris, on the other hand, had to wait much longer to see the new Marguerite: although Sarcey had reported the London success of *La Dame aux Camélias*, it was not until 25 May 1882 that the French capital had a chance to witness Sarah's triumph, when she chose to appear in her acclaimed role for a charity night. In the intervening months Bernhardt toured France – the bookings again arranged by Duquesnel – before resuming in Oc-

tober 1881 her grand tour of Europe, which was to take her as far as Russia.

It was during this period that Sarah became involved in an affair which was as passionate and tragic as those of her stage heroines. Though she disdained completely the image of bourgeois respectability attached to marital status, as her numerous, off-stage romances – a subject for prurient speculation among her biographers – amply testify, she had nevertheless married the Greek diplomat-turned-actor Aristide Damala. Whereas Bernhardt's heroines tended, however tragic the consequences, to fall in love with principled men, Damala was an unscrupulous Casanova, whose profligate habits extended to morphine addiction. It was Bernhardt's sister Jeanne, herself an addict, who had in all probability introduced the pair, with the result that Damala joined Sarah on the 1881–2 tour. The actress, whose better judgement was clouded by her emotions, proceeded to indulge him in the lion's share of the male roles, to the detriment of Angelo and Philippe Garnier, who had helped her plan the tour. Whatever initial stage success Damala enjoyed was merely out of curiosity and publicity rather than talent. His fine masculine physique won him the hearts of female admirers, though not, as it turned out, the laurels of the critics. Acting thoughtlessly and impetuously, Bernhardt made hasty preparations for a marriage, eager to secure her handsome prize. London seemed the most accommodating venue for the union of a Greek Orthodox and a French Catholic of Jewish origin, and the ceremony took place on 4 April 1882. The following month saw the Parisian *première* of *La Dame aux Camélias*, and eager curiosity about the production itself was inevitably matched by the anticipation of witnessing Bernhardt's Marguerite in amorous scenes with Damala's Armand. Just as the real-life affair between Sarah and Mounet-Sully had added piquancy to the earlier Comédie performances, Sarah's recent marriage to a supporting actor added a certain voyeuristic dimension to the onstage intrigue.

Within days of her Parisian début as Marguerite, Sarah returned to London for the fourth year running to give another season at the Gaiety. Damala naturally accompanied her. The London audience was delighted to have its favourite French actress back in the familiar roles of Marguerite, Adrienne,

Froufrou and Doña Sol and was as eager as the Parisians had been for a glimpse of her new partner. For the present, the aura of publicity and curiosity surrounding Damala effectively overshadowed his shortcomings as an actor. The English critics had not been over-enthusiastic about M. Angelo's Armand the previous year, and they were prepared, for the moment at least, to give the newcomer, M. Darall (as Sarah's husband was known professionally), the benefit of the doubt. Towards a performer whose stage experience spanned all of six months, they were ready to be indulgent; the impressive physique undoubtedly played its part, but many thought they could perceive real acting potential besides. Nevertheless, however divided the interest of the audience, critical attention remained firmly focussed on Sarah. There was general concern for her state of health – she was thinner and visibly fatigued owing to the wear and tear of her punishing schedules. In spite of this, her Marguerite continued to enthrall, and her modified interpretation of the death scene (she now leant on Armand, briefly resumed an upright posture, then fell to the ground, clasping her lover's hand the while) was considered more natural and affecting than her original version.

To the established London repertoire Bernhardt now added *Le Sphinx* (in which she took Croizette's former role of Blanche, conferring that of Berthe on her sister) and *Les Faux ménages* by Edouard Pailleron in which she played Esther, a part created by Mme Favart at the Théâtre Français in 1869. Though definitely conceived in a minor key – Esther, unlike Marguerite, is a humble *grisette* rather than a courtesan – the role explored a comparable pathos to that personified in Dumas's heroine in the ostensible conflict between social *déchéance* and inner purity. Favart's interpretation had been somewhat declamatory in a way which fell pleasingly on French ears accustomed to the classical tradition of Corneille and Racine, but Bernhardt's caressing and wheedling accents were more to the taste of the English critics, one of whom commented that 'the grace, beauty, and tenderness of the whole are exquisite, and the method of recitation adds an unspeakable charm to M. Pailleron's ingenious, if rather artificial verses'.[28] Like Thérèse in *Jean-Marie*, Esther moves in a comparatively humble setting, so that Sarah's success in this role would prove that the opulent trappings which invariably surrounded

her heroines of more exalted rank were merely incidental adornments and not, as some had implied, essential to her stage personas:

> For the first time we see this distinguished actress clad in the humble gray dress of an *ouvrière*, the tenant of a shabby lodging in a disreputable quarter. It is needless to say that her art shines no less here than in the boudoir. The part of Esther does not, it is true, afford scope for tempests of passion, but it is full of the tenderness and the gentler emotional effects in which Madame Bernhardt excels.[29]

The part of Esther's lover (another Armand) is not overdemanding, and Damala was sufficiently presentable to make his performance reasonably effective. But he rather overestimated his strengths in the second week when he undertook the lead in *Hernani* and played Sartorys in *Froufrou*. By now the *Era* was objecting to his inability to play anything but Damala, an impression heightened by his insistence on sporting a full beard which prevented him from modifying his appearance in any substantial sense from role to role.[30]

Although the critics were taken with Bernhardt's Esther they were more interested in her portrayal (new to London) of Blanche in *Le Sphinx*, which began the third and final week of the season. Despite her sister's inadequate account of the part of Berthe – it lacked that engaging feminine charm which Bernhardt had so memorably brought to this character – the play provoked a lively following due, in large measure, to Bernhardt's interpretation of Croizette's original role. Despite modifications, her new version of the death scene was hardly less melodramatic than that of her predecessor. Indeed, she contrived to introduce a few of her own grisly embellishments, notably a series of convulsions and facial spasms which, despite the decorous use of a veil, remained horrifyingly visible.

Considering the demands of the European tour and Bernhardt's whirlwind marriage – 'performed so to speak in an *entr'acte*'[31] – it was hardly surprising that the parts of Esther and Blanche were the only new additions to her repertoire. If Sarah, at the age of thirty-seven, had hoped to gain domestic stability from her marriage to nurse the energetic demands of her career, her dreams were all too quickly shattered. Damala's inability to remain faithful or to break his increasingly obvious dependence on morphine resulted in a legal separation in 1883. This was a serious blow to Sarah's pride, and it was the one love affair of her life from which she did not recover easily. Although the two were separated, Sarah's devotion to the profligate actor remained, and the extent of her feeling for Damala, despite their all too brief and stormy passage of love, is demonstrated by her later attempts to help him. For instance, in 1889 when Damala was dying from his addiction, she created the opportunity for him to join her in a final, brief season of performances. It was a magnanimous gesture, which may have boosted Damala's ebbing self-esteem, but it could not save his life. He died in the August of 1889, after the London season they had played together. Thus ended a relationship in which there had been plenty of tragedy but precious little of the romantic.

In any event, it was unlikely that Sarah's life style or temperament could cope with both a career and a long-standing relationship. Neither was it likely that the ego of any lover (and certainly not one as vain and handsome as her husband) would survive being permanently dwarfed by Sarah's great shadow. Aside from Damala's own shortcomings, Sarah herself brought about irreparable damage to her already disintegrating marriage in the autumn of 1882, by embarking on what she clearly sensed would be her next major success, as she entered into collaboration with a playwright who would contribute greatly to her fortunes. Victorien Sardou, a writer with a reputation for prizing quantity above quality in terms of dramatic output, was about to launch Sarah in his *Fédora*, the next major addition to her repertoire. It was an event which would serve to close the private chapter of marriage, but which would open a new phase in Sarah's stage career.

## Notes

1. *Daily Telegraph*, 25 May 1880.
2. *The Times*, 26 May 1880.
3. *Daily Telegraph*, 27 May 1880.

4. *Theatre*, 1 July 1880, p. 27.
5. *Daily Telegraph*, 27 May 1880.
6. *Pall Mall Gazette*, 27 May 1880.
7. *Morning Post*, 27 May 1880.
8. *Morning Post* , 28 May 1880.
9. *Pall Mall Gazette*, 29 May 1880.
10. *Theatre*, 1 July 1880, p. 56.
11. *Morning Post*, 1 June 1880.
12. *Morning Post*, 11 June 1880.
13. *Era*, 20 June 1880.
14. *Pall Mall Gazette*, 21 June 1880.
15. Sarah Bernhardt, *Mémoires*, vol. II, pp. 148–9.
16. Ibid., p. 282.
17. Louis Verneuil, *The Fabulous Life of Sarah Bernhardt*, trans. Ernest Boyd (New York & London: Harper, 1942), p. 99.
18. *The Times*, 13 June 1881.
19. *Pall Mall Gazette*, 13 June 1881.
20. *Daily Telegraph*, 13 June 1881.
21. Francisque Sarcey, *Quarante ans de théâtre*, 8 vols (Paris: Bibliothèque des Annales, 1900–2), vol. V, p. 196.
22. *Morning Post*, 13 June 1881.
23. *Pall Mall Gazette*, 13 June 1881.
24. *Pall Mall Gazette*, 7 June 1880.
25. *Daily News*, 13 June 1881.
26. *Pall Mall Gazette*, 13 June 1881.
27. *Era*, 25 June 1881.
28. *Pall Mall Gazette*, 3 June 1882.
29. *The Times*, 3 June 1882.
30. *Era*, 10 June 1882.
31. *The Times*, 30 May 1882.

*Plate 1.* Sarah Bernhardt aged twelve and her mother, *Strand Magazine,*
April 1904

*Plate 2.* Sarah Bernhardt as Marguerite in *La Dame aux Camélias*; premièred in London, 1881, Enthoven Collection

*Plate 3.* Sarah Bernhardt as Lady Macbeth at the Gaiety Theatre,
July 1884, photograph by Nadar, Enthoven Collection

*Plate 4.* Sarah Bernhardt as Tosca, premièred in Paris 1887, photograph by Nadar (*Théâtre Complet*, vol 1, 1934, Sardou)

*Plate 5.* Sarah Bernhardt, Portrait Photograph by Nadar, c. 1889,
Enthoven Collection

*Plate 6.* Sarah Bernhardt as Hamlet, 1899 (*Beyond the Footlights*, 1904, Mrs Alec-Tweedie)

*Plate 7.* Frontispiece for Sarah Bernhardt's version of *Adrienne Lecouvreur*, published 1908

*Plate 8.* Prime Minister William Gladstone at Sarah Bernhardt's Art Exhibition, London, 1879, *Strand Magazine*, September 1904

# 4 Sardou

Sarah's success and the recognition of her talent had spread through countries and continents. Wherever she travelled and performed she was fêted and applauded on an international scale. As she prepared to embark on what was to be a new phase, and by the same token a new success in her career, she had also to think of the two men in her life, Maurice and Damala, who were enjoying little wealth and less happiness. Unfortunately, neither of the strategies devised by Sarah for promoting her son and husband proved propitious. She purchased the Théâtre de l'Ambigu for Maurice, whose inexperience of theatre management did not bode well for the first production, *Les Mères ennemis* by Catulle Mendès, in November 1882. The play was lavishly and expensively mounted and had a talented cast, but failed to prove popular with audiences. The failing was largely the fault of Maurice's mismanagement, but equally Sarah's attempts to transform a theatre which had housed popular drama into a venue for more literary endeavours could not be achieved overnight, and certainly not without her own glittering presence, which the public had mistakenly expected to see in the production.

Equally disastrous was the project of establishing Damala in the leading role at the Ambigu, which was intended to compensate for his having failed to obtain the part of Loris Ipanoff in *Fédora*, a role which fell to Pierre Berton when the play opened at the Vaudeville on 12 December 1882. Whether Sardou had refused to have Damala's inadequate talent ruin his production, or whether Sarah herself had envisaged his inclusion in the cast as an unwise step, is unclear. What is certain is that the popularity of *Fédora* totally overshadowed the *succès d'estime* of the Ambigu venture, causing an angry Damala to desert the production.

*Fédora* was less popular with the drama critics, even though their dissenting voices did not deter the audiences, who continued to flock to the Vaudeville, ensuring a successful run lasting until

April 1883. However, Bernhardt's box-office success at the Vaudeville was not enough to compensate for the Ambigu disaster, or rather disasters, for the second production, *La Glu* by Jean Richepin, was also a costly failure. The blame lay with the management rather than the cast. Sarah's choice of dramatist and play showed that her own theatrical interests were much wider than the repertoire with which she was associated but that these experiments were incompatible with popular tastes. That such an obviously weak drama should have been staged at all was due to Richepin's amorous advances, which were consoling Bernhardt for the loss of Damala. Richepin may have had some success in ministering to Sarah's emotional needs, but his drama, dedicated to her, did nothing to improve her financial affairs. It was necessary to hold a sale of her jewellery in February 1883 in order to pay for Maurice's mistakes and her own choice of repertoire which had, in total, left her with a debt of 400,000 francs.

Because of her financial reversals in Paris, it was essential that Bernhardt recoup her losses, hopefully by means of a successful and lucrative London season at the Gaiety. Mayer and Hollingshead were also in need of a box-office success, owing to the poor attendances of the French summer season prior to Sarah's opening night on 9 July 1883. As a result, the seats for her performances were twice the customary tariff. Sarah's London public, undeterred by these inflated prices, booked their seats for her nine performances, given between 9 and 14 July, well in advance. This heavy demand meant, as *The Times* reviewer pointed out, that speculators were able to offload tickets 'at fancy prices,'[1] and Sarah was assured of her packed houses.

London audiences were already familiar with the plot of *Fédora*, either through the Paris theatre column reports of the original production or because they had attended Mrs Bernard-Beere's performance in an English version at the Haymarket earlier in May. In no way, however, did this detract from the enthusiasm and interest aroused by the prospect of seeing Bernhardt in the role.

Briefly, the four-act, Sardou drama centres on the Russian princess Fédora, whose husband-to-be, Wladimir, has been murdered as the curtain rises. What ensues is Fédora's quest for vengeance. Love and revenge collide and conflict, as the assassin she seeks arouses her passion. Political intrigue and the misuse of partial knowledge complicate the chain of unfortunate events, in which Fédora inadvertently heaps misfortune upon her lover and his family. To atone for her sins Fédora takes poison and dies in agony but, in a state of redemption, in the arms of her lover.

Fédora was the first of several parts which Sardou tailored to fit Bernhardt's personality and, above all, to suit her essential femininity. The hallmark of these roles was their range of emotion; they afforded Sarah the opportunity of running up and down the scales of love, from notes of tenderness to chords of electric passion. Furthermore, these were roles of women in possession of social power, whose wealth and standing demanded great and deep, if hopeless, liaisons. In the case of Fédora this was admirably demonstrated by Sarah in the second act (the opening scenes having set the revenge quest in motion), in which, as the *Daily Telegraph* reviewer commented, the 'two sides to Fédora', her 'power and passion', collide.[2]

The following act provides the high point in terms of dramatic tension, as Fédora, by degrees, realises the web of misfortune she has woven and the conflicting passions which have overtaken her. The battle between love and knowledge crescendos in scene six of the third act, as Fédora listens to her lover's true account of the murder. Because Fédora is the silent listener, Bernhardt's depiction of anguish and passion was externalised by means of facial and bodily gestures:

> With fixed and dazed look Fédora heard the explanations which, while it left her heart free to honour whom it loved, opened out for her a dim vision of the possible consequences of her mad haste. Purely womanly was the rage with which the letters betraying the falsehood of her slain lover were crumpled, torn, and scattered to the winds. Then came a scene of irresistible seductiveness in which to save the life of Loris she heaped upon him every form of caress, and wooed him to strength with the wiles of a Cleopatra.[3]

For the final act Sardou had created a harrowing death scene which again afforded Sarah the opportunity to draw on her emotional prowess, as the young princess resigns herself to her fate, expiring in the arms of her lover.

In this London production Bernhardt made various changes to the original. In a directorial capacity, Sarah had a keen eye for the pictorial potential of her stage tableaux and would often make changes, not simply to suit her own images and movements, but also to improve the overall aesthetic impact of a scene. The changes to *Fédora* met with varying degrees of approval. In the opening act, the death scene of Wladimir had taken place off-stage, behind closed doors, in accordance with Sardou's directions. Sarah now incorporated an opening of the doors to an alcove, in order to reveal a distraught Fédora, wailing at the side of Wladimir's death bed. Despite audience enthusiasm for this piece of stage-craft, the critics in general considered that the additional note of realism detracted from the tenor of tragic dignity. Similarly Sarah altered the climax of the second act. Originally, Loris (Berton) had left the stage, and alone Sarah delivered the ironic line, 'Ah! bandit! Je te tiens!' This was replaced by a tableau of Fédora and Loris together, the curtain falling on the princess shuddering at the handclasp of her assassin-lover. The alterations show that Sarah sought to concentrate on the visual dimension of performances in her English productions and that this gave her some scope for a directorial input which, as her frustrated literary endeavours at the Ambigu indicate, she was keen to develop.

Despite the acknowledged sensationalism of such alterations, overall, critics and audiences alike were thrilled by her emotionalist style. The actress and character were as one. Charmed by the 'magic of her musical voice' and the 'spontaneousness of inspiration', the reviewer for *The Times* opined that the 'emotions of the actress' were not 'simulated, but felt'.[4] The tears she shed in the final throes of agony seemed to be real tears, as were those of her audience, weeping copiously as the final curtain fell. Although Bernhardt's figure had filled out considerably since her first London visit and though the 'golden voice' showed signs of performance strain, exacerbated by the effects of a cold, the magic was still as spell-binding as ever. For English audiences, Sardou's contrived Bernhardt-show-case-plays were not at issue. Sarah's performance was the play.

The play was, in fact, such a success that the original plans for the season were cancelled in favour of *Fédora*. The scheduled programme was to have included Richepin's *Pierrot assassin*, a pantomime devised at the Trocadéro in April 1883, and one of her Comédie début roles, the heroine in Scribe's *Valérie*, which she had toured in the spring. Both of these were cancelled, and all nine performances were given over to *Fédora*. Sarah did, however, give a private, late-night performance of *Valérie* at the New Club, Covent Garden, on the Saturday of her departure from the capital (14 July), in which she recreated the title role of the blind girl, originally played by Mlle Mars, thereby adding another convincing and realistic portrait of blindness to that of her sightless Posthumia.

Sarah's second major box-office hit with Sardou came to London two summers later when *Théodora* opened at the Gaiety, 11 July 1885. The play was first produced in December 1884 at the Porte Saint-Martin. It was to this theatre that Bernhardt had transferred her managerial interests after the Ambigu disasters. She had again installed Maurice as manager, under the guidance of Derembourg, who soon afterwards was financially ousted and replaced by Sarah's old friend and mentor, Félix Duquesnel, in the autumn of 1884.

The period between the London production of *Fédora* and of *Théodora* had again proved disastrous for Sarah, both artistically and personally. Sarah was approaching forty, and both her career and her love life seemed set on a downward trend. Her love affair with Richepin was as unfortunate and as unsuccessful as her programme of productions, and their amorous association proved incapable of surviving the impact of their joint artistic disasters. He had been supportive in coming to her aid over the scurrilous publication. *The Life and Memoirs of Sarah Barnum*, issued from the vitriolic pen of fellow actress, Marie Colombier. The publication used a fictional, grotesque, impresario 'Barnum' figure (but who was clearly and unmistakably meant to be Sarah) for the purpose of character assassination. Richepin had contributed to the scandal surrounding the publication by being party to a physical assault on the authoress instigated by Sarah and supported also by Maurice. This did not, however, compensate in Sarah's eyes for the failure of his *Nana Sahib*, played in May 1884. The play was greeted with little enthusiasm, and what little there was was generated not by the play itself but by the scandal surrounding the memoir publication. To make matters worse, Damala had made a surprising comeback, and was partnering Jane Hading at the Gymnase in the leading role in *Le Maître de Forges*, the one and only veritable success of his stage career. So while Bernhardt and Richepin (who was also appearing in his own production) played to empty houses, Damala was reaping the benefits of a long and successful run. The termination of Richepin's liaison with Bernhardt was finally precipitated by his unsuccessful adaptation of *Macbeth*. Premièred in Paris in May 1884, it was then audaciously transferred to London for the summer season. In neither capital was it a success.

As with the Ambigu venture, Sarah was finding that audiences at the Porte Saint-Martin, again a theatre with a history of melodrama and spectacle, were unwilling to support her more 'artistic' endeavours. In view of these failures, Sarah again needed to revive her artistic, financial and spiritual fortunes. Sardou's *Théodora* provided her with a drama on a grand scale suited to the Porte Saint-Martin audiences. Duquesnel's directorial capacity for spectacle ensured a sumptuous and successful staging, and Sarah, as a consequence, was provided with the means to set her affairs in order.

In his composition of *Théodora*, Sardou had surpassed himself in the design of a Bernhardt-vehicle, not least because Théodora mirrored Sarah's own exotic, Parisian personality. The courtesan–gipsy turned Byzantine empress combined love, power and the spirit of the *demi-monde*, redolent, despite the play's historical exotica, of the Second Empire. As in *Fédora*, political intrigue complicates the stage action, though it again constitutes an unnecessary, cumbersome and unwelcome addition to the drama of the love-triangle. Nevertheless, Théodora's secret passion for Andréas, would-be assassin of her husband–emperor, Justinien, provides the occasion for a thrilling dramatic climax to the stage action. As the assassination plot is discovered, Théodora is forced to kill a trapped conspirator, Marcellus, in order to protect her lover. Horror ensues as Andréas discovers Théodora's true identity. A further twist in the plot sends Andréas to his death at the hands of Théodora, as she administers poison, believing it to be a love potion. Now that the emperor has discovered his wife's infidelity, she too is sentenced to death, and the curtain falls on a

Théodora crouched over the body of her lover, as she awaits her own execution. Though more deviant and less innocent than Fédora, the Byzantine empress shares with the Russian princess a Cleopatra-like view of the world, that of a life which is not worth living without her Antony.

The Byzantine setting was lavishly mounted. Sarah had travelled to Italy to make a study of the church of San Vitale in Ravenna, from which she had devised her ideas for the costumes and scenery. Though the sets had been chastened since the Paris production, they and the costumes had been renovated and renewed at Mayer's expense. Such an outlay dispelled any thought of reneging on the French summer seasons, a possibility that had been quietly fermenting since the poor attendances in the early part of the 1883 season.

The play opened to great applause on one of the hottest nights of an exceptionally warm July and was repeated exclusively on evenings between 11 and 24 July 1885. On the opening night the play lasted for over four hours, though the heat and the longevity of the programme did not dampen the enthusiasm of a brilliant first night audience, which included the Prince and Princess of Wales, eager for the return of their favourite French actress.

Bernhardt, as she made her first appearance, was attired in a 'close-clinging costume of embroidered silk and satin and golden cloth heavy with precious stones, and with low-girt belt',[5] which she had copied from one of the church mosaics. In her hand she carried white lilies, to complete the image of sumptuous luxury and satiety. This contrasted starkly with her next appearance in more sombre dress and with veiled visage, as her *nostalgie de la boue* took her out into the streets, away from the pomp and circumstance of the court.

As a reward for patiently persevering with the tortuous details of Sardou's political sub-plot, the audience was treated to a thrilling scene of dramatic irony. While Théodora/Myrtha is ensconced in the arms of Andréas, he joins in the chorus of a revolutionary song directed against the empress, not knowing that the woman he loves and the woman he decries are one and the same:

Languid, voluptuous, and wearied in the opening scene, she exposes in the following a frank gaiety of Bohemian nature, the effect of which is irresistible. Then comes the lovemaking with Andréas, such lovemaking as Madame Sarah Bernhardt alone can show. Coaxing and passionate in turns, cooing tenderly with bird-like notes, full of witchery and variety as Cleopatra herself, she holds and subjugates the austere and ambitious man to whose love she has stooped. When she hears him murmuring with enthusiasm the chorus descriptive of her own infamy the various phases of anger and consternation are superbly shown, and she claps her hand on the loved mouth to prevent the repetition of so treasonable an utterance.[6]

In terms of dramatic tension and suspense, the scene parallels act three, scene six, of *Fédora*, as Loris Ipanoff unwittingly denounces the princess as the instrument of his destruction. From a position of complete knowledge, the audience, in both of these scenes, was able to decode the interchanging notes of consternation, concealment and passion gesturally conveyed by Sarah.

In terms of suspense technique, however, the ironic content of this tableau was surpassed by the torture scene of act three, in which Théodora must find the resolve to kill Marcellus. Though Sardou's scripting of the scene is, as some reviewers indicated,[7] potentially melodramatic, Sarah's art raised it to the heights of tragic grandeur. Likewise, this was the note on which she brought the action to a close, in a final magnificent and emotional tableau: 'When she flings the pearls from her neck, and bares it for the cord which the executioner twists round it as the curtain falls, the actress reaches the full height of her art; for one moment she arouses us to the required "pity and fear", and the drama touches the line of tragedy.'[8]

Though recognising the note of tragic dignity in the closure of the action, the *Spectator*, along with several of the other reviewers, also cast a critical eye over both the play and the actress. At one level, the sensation and scale of the drama and the performance were undeniable; at another, it opened up a debate on the dangers of formulaic drama and stereotyped characterisation. Although on the one hand, the failure of the drama in London predicted by the Paris·critics did not arise,[9] Sarah's future in such roles was seriously questioned. The wisdom, or rather the folly, of an overindulged poetic licence in the treatment of an historical subject came under close scrutiny, as did Sarah's composition of the Sardou-heroine. Accusations of a modern manner and prosaic speech, conflicting with the need for a classical restraint, tone and verse in the dramatisation of the historical subject, were akin to the type of modern, cinematic criticisms frequently levelled at the Hollywood Epic. Furthermore, the epic proportions of *Théodora* were, in part, reduced by the smallness of the Gaiety stage, which notably hampered scenes such as the torturing of Marcellus, when the performers were in such close proximity to each other that it was impossible to give credence to the notion that Théodora's encounter with the conspirator was not overheard by Justinien and his entourage.[10]

As to Sarah's emotionalist style in this production, criticisms pointed towards a tendency in her performance to be overstepping the limitations of the Sardou formula. The love, the burning ardour, the anguish of the heroine's dilemma and downfall were bordering on self-caricature. Hence, superlative praise for the role, which on the one hand was heralded as one which posterity might possibly acclaim as one of her 'most memorable', was countered on the other by the detection of an 'overdone' method, a style which threatened to 'lapse into mannerism'.[11] Significantly, amongst those numbered in the first night audience were Mr J.C. Toole's company, who were presumably eager for further study of the Bernhardt mannerisms to perfect for their latest burlesque venture, *The O'dora: or the Wrong Accent*. Devised by F.C. Burnard, this burlesque provided actress Marie Linden with the opportunity of displaying her skills at caricaturing the great actress, though if the London critics are to be believed in the summer of 1885, Bernhardt was having little trouble in achieving this herself.

Courtesy of *Théodora*'s financial successes, Sarah, back at the Porte Saint-Martin, was able to concentrate on an artistic rather than a commercial venture, in the form of a Hugo revival. The December production of *Marion Delorme*, designed as a tribute to the author who had died that year, did not prove popular, and before long Sarah was once more touring on a global scale, taking in North and South America, in order to fill depleted coffers.[12] Jarrett, the impresario who first arranged her American tours, died during the 1886-7 tour and was replaced in this capacity by Sarah's secretary, Maurice Grau.[13] Both on the outward voyage

65

in the late spring of 1886 and on her summer return in 1887, Sarah stopped off in London to perform stock-in-trade favourites from her repertoire. Not until the summer of 1888 did she cap her earlier, Sardou successes and finally allay the critical fears of the 1885 season with her performance as the tragic opera singer in *La Tosca*.

When *La Tosca* was premièred at the Porte Saint-Martin, 24 November 1887, the Bernhardt production was again panned by the French press. Their hostility was due in no small measure to Sarah's refusal to have the press present at her final dress rehearsal. The on-going hostility between the French star and her native press produced the customary predictions of failure mingled with a disparaging view of English and American theatrical tastes, in the event of it succeeding abroad. The *Pall Mall Gazette*, for example, reported on Francisque Sarcey's denunciation and revilement of Sardou. 'Sarcey', the reviewer wrote, 'accused him [Sardou] of prostituting his muse for filthy lucre, and producing a "mere article of exportation" fit only for ignorant Englishmen and American savages'.[14] Although the generality of English reviewers shared in the admonition of Sardou as a playwright, the stage-craft and Sarah's performance in *La Tosca* were valued as a contribution to the theatrical canon.

Set in Rome in 1800 on the eve of the Battle of Marengo, the play introduces the prima donna, Floria Tosca, passionately and jealously in love with Mario Cavardossi (Dumeny). Political intrigue is more happily interwoven with desire in *La Tosca* than in *Théodora*. Mario's republican sympaties involve him in helping a fellow republican, Angelotti, to escape the chief of police, Baron Scarpia (Berton). Irrationally driven by her jealous love, Tosca unwittingly leads Scarpia to Mario and Angelotti. As Scarpia tortures Mario for information regarding Angelotti's whereabouts, a desperate Tosca reveals the details. The fourth act contains Sarah's famous stabbing scene, as Tosca consents to Scarpia's advances in return for Mario's freedom. When she believes Scarpia has agreed to her terms, she stabs him, only to discover in the final act that Mario has already been killed, leaving Tosca to leap to her own watery grave from the battlements of St Angelo prison.

Though seat prices had again doubled for Bernhardt's London

performances of *La Tosca*, she opened to a full house which stayed for the duration of the long performance, despite the fact that this entailed missing the suburban trains and omnibuses. The highlights of the evening's entertainment were clearly the torture scene of the third act and the stabbing of Scarpia in the fourth. Though nerves made Sarah's opening scenes somewhat rapid in delivery, she returned to her spell-binding magnetism in the third:

> The voice strangled with sobs, the piteous wails of despair, the dishevelled and tangled hair of the wretched woman, her heart cries, her agonised beatings at her prison bars, her utter prostration and demoralisation whilst her lover was exhorting her to valour through her groans, made up a memory of this actress that will scarcely be forgotten – not a pleasant memory, but an indelible one. The excitement during this scene, and after it, was tremendous. Women who listened became choked with emotion, even men turned pale with the effect of highly-strained imagination.[15]

It was generally considered that the blatant brutality of this scene, particularly the appearance of the heavily blood-stained Mario stumbling on to the stage, could have been tempered to avoid the hysteria it caused amongst the female members of the audience. Consequently, the stabbing scene, which roused the spectators to new heights of breathless emotion, was reviewed and assessed as a more brilliant piece of stage-craft, particularly with respect to Sarah's movements. The stabbing was followed by an administration of the last rites which necessitated the setting out of two candles by Scarpia's head and the laying of a crucifix on his breast. The Protestant English audience failed to grasp Tosca's Catholic reverence for the dead, despite the violent deeds, and were more inclined to nervous laughter than the Catholic Parisian spectators had been. Though a long, demanding and arduous part, it afforded Sarah the opportunity for displaying the best of her talents, and on this occasion, she did not fall short of the role requirements:

> The first act is given up to feline tenderness and half-sportive, half-passionate erotics. The second act shows us the petted artist and the jealous woman. In the third she goes through a crisis of mortal agony such has scarcely been attempted on the stage. In the fourth she rises

from stony stupor to avenging fury; and in the fifth the note of love is touched once more only to pass over instantaneously into horror and despair. A more exhausting part has never fallen to the lot of any actress; but the effect is correspondingly intense.[16]

Judged in terms of the histrionic style, some reviewers were inclined to credit the performance as unsurpassable. Interestingly, the *Era* was urging the up-and-coming generation of playgoers to see her emotionalist method, while she was visiting London.[17] An interview with the *Era* gave Sarah the opportunity to reinforce her objection to Coquelin's 'double personality theory', that is to say, the actress in dual role of performer and critical observer of her own acts and to confirm her emotionalist theory of performance in which the responses of both audience and actor are directly engaged. When asked if anti Diderot's concept of the paradox of the actor (as set out in his anti-emotionalist treatise of 1830, *Le Paradoxe sur le comédien*, from which Coquelin et al. took their cue) she replied, 'Absolutely. I actually feel everything my character is supposed to feel. I shed tears on the stage every night when my "personage" weeps. At Marseilles a month or two ago in the third act of *La Tosca*, at the moment she is supposed to faint, I fainted in real earnest.'[18]

The success of *Fédora*, *Théodora* and *La Tosca* can only be judged and understood in terms of Bernhardt's histrionic method. Sardou merely provided the framework from which Sarah was able to demonstrate the finest effects of her acting style, and the greatest of these was her portrait of modern love. However exotic or remote the settings and subjects of these dramas, her portrayal of the heroine engaged in the archetypal, ill-fated love-quest was entirely modern in its conception. The method of placing the heroine in a male world of political intrigue, of which she had only partial knowledge, meant that the female world of love, though destined for destruction, was paradoxically viewed as triumphing over the forces which destroyed it. Recourse to dramatic irony, manifest in the use of female accoutrements which prove fatal to the lovers (the fan in *La Tosca* which incites the heroine's jealousy; the letter in *Fédora* which links Loris to the crime and the 'love' potion in *Théodora* which kills Andréas) is a commonly enforced technique precisely because it sharpens the emotional response of both the performer and the audience. Similarly, the identity of the heroine as public figure and woman in love mirrored, compounded and intensified Sarah's own image of star actress and off-stage mistress of tempestuous, romantic attachments, to the extent that all three heroines, in a sense, were simply facets of the Bernhardt personality cult.

In reality Sarah was now a middle-aged woman, but in the main this was not how audiences and critics 'saw' her. With the aid of the press and her own propensity for self-advertisement, Sarah had successfully created an all-encompassing image of seductress. She had permitted and even to an extent encouraged or condoned her 'private life' being transformed into another factional spectacle. In the public eye, Sarah was as legendary and seductive as the heroines she played, but she had created a difficulty for herself in choosing, furthering and promoting a fixed and frozen image at odds with the reality of an aging woman and the rigors of a consistently demanding profession.

The dangers of writing purely for the histrionic method are already sign-posted in the Sardou dramas of the 1880s. The restrictions of their formulaic construction are further underlined by a brief examination of Sardou's later vehicles for Sarah, in which he tried unsuccessfully to temper and modify the melodramatic strategies, with a view to variety, and in order to provide Sarah with roles better suited to her maturity. Leaving aside Sardou's production of *Cléopâtre*, which thematically belongs to the next chapter, there remain three Sardou plays which were included in later London seasons, namely *Gismonda*, *Spiritisme* and *La Sorcière*.

*Gismonda*, included in the repertoire of plays in the summer of 1895, is set in a duchy of fifteenth-century Athens. The intrigue centres on the Duchess, Gismonda, whose child is rescued from danger by a low-born Athenian, Almeiro. At the moment of danger, Gismonda promised her hand in marriage to the saviour of her child and is therefore rashly committed to a marriage beneath her station. When Almeiro will not release her from her promise, she bargains for her freedom by offering one night of passion, though subsequently she realises the nobility of his nature and consents to their union before her assembled people. En route, the complication of the action is such that Gismonda, *in extremis*, is forced to strike an evil suitor to death with a hatchet. The way in which this differs from the bloody deeds of *Théodora* or *La Tosca* is in the motivation of a maternal rather than a sexual love. Gismonda's love for Almeiro comes by degrees of realisation, without Tosca's jealous furies, and it is concern for her son rather than for herself which constitutes the mainspring of the play's action. Similarly, it is the image of the mother-figure which is presented as a final, closing tableau, rather than the harrowing last moments of a young, victim-heroine. As the action culminated in a Palm-Sunday procession in a Byzantine church, complete with priests, congregation candles, incense and flowers, Bernhardt made use of the setting to present Gismonda and her son in a Madonna and Child tableau. Though such effects were picturesque and touching, it was to the flashes of the former passionate heroine which the audience turned for dramatic interest. The greatest of these was Gismonda's conversion to Almeiro in the third act:

> this is the one overpowering episode in the play, and it is treated by Madame Bernhardt with a sympathetic skill which takes every spectator captive. The few sentences in which Gismonda acknowledges the nobility of Almeiro, and confesses the extent to which her heart is touched, are spoken by the actress in a fashion which can only be described as exquisite.[19]

Compared to Tosca, the role of Gismonda is comparatively slight, and there was not sufficient opportunity for Bernhardt to take command of a performance which had too many trappings and not enough substance. The fact that the scenic trappings also detracted from the action, in so far as the elaborate locales – which included a view of the Acropolis, the interior of a convent, the Duchess's chamber and the Byzantine church – took a long time to shift, did little to smooth over the inadequacies of dramatic composition. Not enough consideration had been given to the transference of scenery from the Théâtre de la Renaissance, which Sarah had taken over in 1893, to Daly's, leased for her summer season.[20] Consequently the audience spent a good deal of time between the acts, in darkness, waiting for the scene changes. On the first night especially, the final curtain did not come down before 12:30, and on this occasion, many spectators left before the end, whilst the gallery boys voiced audience sentiments, with a rendition of 'We won't go home 'til morning'.

*Spiritisme* was performed in London in the summer of 1897. Like *Gismonda*, it too came from Sarah's Renaissance repertoire. Premièred in Paris on 3 February 1897, *Spiritisme* was a crushing failure, and it is hard to understand why Sarah should have included it in her London season at the Adelphi. As in the case of *Gismonda* at Daly's, Sarah would have been well-advised to have checked on the adaptability of *Spiritisme* for the Adelphi. Complaints of inaudability suggested an inadequate consideration of the Adelphi accoustics.[21]

Set in the France of the day, *Spiritisme* offers the implausible and improbable action of an adulterous wife who effected a reconciliation with her husband by reappearing as a 'spirit' to test his forgiveness, which was ultimately granted. The theme provoked facetious comments from reviewers, such as the question from the *Star* reviewer who asked, 'if the husband believes in spiritualism after this, he must be a wonder. For what is the good of table-rapping that tells you to look out of a window and neglects to tell you that your wife has run away with a lover?'[22] Though Sarah could generally overcome mediocre playwrighting by means of her histrionic talent, she could not rescue *Spiritisme*. Despite the play being an ill-conceived, shallow piece of nonsense, Sarah might have succeeded in triumphing over the odds of bad playwrighting, if Sardou's heroine, Simone D'Aubenas, had possessed something of the Magdalen spirit, which redeems a woman like Théodora:

> The character of the blasé woman of the world is conveyed by a variety of subtle little touches, and she has pathetic tones as penetrating as ever. But how is it possible to be moved at the distresses of such a huzzy as the author has been at such pains to depict or of her amiable but rather ridiculous husband, who bores his friends on the slightest provocation with commonplaces on the subject of life and futurity.[23]

The reviewer might also have added the conception of the lover, Valentin, who, unlike Andréas or Loris, is a thorough rogue. Chastity is not a prerequisite of a Bernhardt heroine, but an underlying 'goodness' of spirit is, just as nobility must be a

71

hallmark of the hero-lover. Consequently, the play survived for a mere three performances in London. For once, the English critics came out in support of their French counterparts.

Sardou returned to the theme of the occult in his last play for Sarah, *La Sorcière*. Given the failings of *Spiritisme*, he returned, for one last time, to the large, operatic scale of *Théodora* or *La Tosca*. The play had its first successful run at the Théâtre Sarah Bernhardt (formerly the Théâtre des Nations), where it opened on 15 December 1903. This was the Parisian theatre which Sarah managed after the Renaissance in 1899, and in the tradition of successful actress-managers, named the theatre after herself as a monument to her achievements. One of the main reasons for Sarah's acquisition of this venue was its size, which could accommodate both a large audience (which meant increased box-office receipts) and elaborate scene setting. Hence it was suited to Sardou's *La Sorcière*, which treated the persecution of the Moorish sorceress Zoraya and contained all the grand elements of the earlier, melodramatic formula: seduction, thwarted love, martyrdom and tragic dénouement.

When transferred to London in the summer of 1904, however, reviews testify that for English audiences, the old formula no longer thrilled as it had done in the 1880s. The role presented Sarah with plenty of opportunity for displays of 'beauty', but the old 'strength' and fieriness were missing,[24] particularly as Sarah was considerably older by this time. The passionate ardour of a heroine like Tosca could not be substituted, it would seem, by a maternal Gismonda, an adulterous Simone or a widowed Zoraya.

Sarah's performances in the early Sardou plays had served a paradigmatic purpose with regard to her emotionalist method and at the same time had engaged the actress in the closed discourse of ill-fated heroine. The later attempts to adapt and modify this formula simply confirm its immutability. Trapped within the self-created image of martyred femininity, Sarah could either choose to exploit the archetype in other artistic ventures or attempt to find an alternative. An examination of other 'saints' and 'sinners' from the middle phase of Bernhardt's career will show how these directions were explored and received.

# Notes

1. *The Times*, 10 July 1883.
2. *Daily Telegraph*, 10 July 1883.
3. *Morning Post*, 10 July 1883.
4. *The Times*, 10 July 1883.
5. *Daily News*, 13 July 1885.
6. *Morning Post*, 13 July 1885.
7. See *Daily Telegraph*, 13 July 1885.
8. *Spectator*, 18 July 1885.
9. See *Era*, 18 July 1885.
10. See *Spectator*, 18 July 1885.
11. *Theatre*, August 1885.
12. Huret *Sarah Bernhardt: acteurs et actrices d'aujourd'hui* (Paris: Juven, 1899), p. 68 cites Bernhardt's personal profits from the South American tour as 1,500,000 francs.
13. See William Emboden, *Sarah Bernhardt* (London: Studio Vista, Macmillan, 1974), p. 78.
14. *Pall Mall Gazette*, 10 July 1888.
15. *Daily Telegraph*, 10 July 1888.
16. *Pall Mall Gazette*, 10 July 1888.
17. *Era*, 14 July 1888.
18. *Era*, 21 July 1888.
19. *Morning Post*, 28 May 1895.
20. Sarah's management of the Renaissance Theatre lasted from November 1893 until January 1899.
21. See *Star*, 7 July 1897.
22. Ibid.
23. *Daily News*, 7 July 1897.
24. *The Times*, 21 June 1904.

# 5 Saints and Sinners

Despite the scepticism which had first coloured the attitude of the French critics to Sarah's skills as a tragedienne, the actress had proceeded to demonstrate a talent for combining the popular style of the Boulevard with the Classical tradition of the Comèdie Française to create a highly pictorial but successful portrayal of a Racinian heroine. It was true that the pantomimic agonies of Sarah's Phèdre were a far cry from Rachel's statuesque and majestic decline, but they constituted an electrifying and radical interpretation. Once Sarah had proved she could master the rigors of Phèdre, she continued to extend her repertoire of tragic women in the 1880s and 1890s by undertaking certain of the heroines from Shakespeare's tragedies. During her apprenticeship at the Odéon in 1868 she had performed the role of Cordelia with success, though this had not been repeated in any of her London seasons. At the Comédie Française she had performed the fifth act of *Othello*, playing Desdemona to Mounet-Sully's farcically excessive Moor (27 February 1878). Again, this had not been reworked when Sarah had seen fit to start out on her own.

The first opportunity that London audiences had of seeing Sarah perform in one of the Shakespeare tragedies was in the 1884 *Macbeth* project with Richepin. Her keen interest in *Macbeth* was made apparent when she performed the sleep-walking scene on a benefit evening for Mme Fargueil at the Vaudeville (8 November 1883), prior to the full-length Paris production of the tragedy. Curiosity mounted as news of Sarah's intention to play Lady Macbeth in the forthcoming London season reached the English critics. Just as the French press had been anxious to see how Sarah would play Phèdre, the English reviewers were now equally aroused – and more than a little concerned – at the prospect of seeing her Shakespeare heroine. They were not, on this occasion, going to be content to dismiss the text and concentrate entirely on Sarah's performance. Sardou's melodramatic playwrighting could be readily dismissed by the English critics as a problem for the French dramatic canon, but they were sensitive to any treatment of their own great playwright. Analysis of Richepin's prose translation of *Macbeth* revealed a woefully inadequate rendition of the bard's tragic verse. Sarah had first attempted to secure the translation by Jules Lacroix (1863) but had failed to obtain his permission for a revival before the end of the Porte Saint-Martin season.[1] Richepin was then under orders to produce a new version. That the translation had been accomplished as a hurried response to Sarah's request is demonstrably clear from the writing. Richepin's literal prose translation (indicative of melodrama rather than tragedy) was a very poor substitute for the rhythmic quality of the Shakespearean verse. As evidence of the drama's weak and literal composition, critics cited the witches' scene 'which in plain prose', wrote one, 'sounds like the parody of a cookery book, and provokes roars of laughter'.[2]

Sarah took the *Macbeth* production to Edinburgh in an attempt to infuse some local colour into the drabness of Richepin's writing and then travelled down to the English capital. That she herself had reservations about the production is reflected in the London programme. She performed *Fédora* from Monday to Thursday of her first week and held *Macbeth* in reserve until the Friday and Saturday (4 and 5 July). During the four-week season it was given only one more performance (19 July), the remainder of the programme consisting solely of safe box-office draws: *Fédora*, *Froufrou*, *Ruy Blas* and *Adrienne Lecouvreur*.

Because Scotland's capital was privileged to receive the production before London, English expectations were intensified all the more and compounded to an even greater degree by the advance publicity:

> Long before last night the photograph of the new Lady Macbeth had appeared in the shop windows, representing her as a maiden of Joan of Arc pattern with long fair hair bound with a fillet or semi-crown, an elastic breast-plate – or, to put it less romantically, a jersey – adorned with the emblem of the fleur de lys, a girdle and a pleated white garment which clung mysteriously to the figure.[3]

Sarah's contour-hugging garment, which replaced the 'queenly robes' traditionally worn by English actresses in the part, puzzled some critics. The choice of costume, however, was a

75

further instance of Sarah's conscious attempt to highlight an image of seductive and fatal womanhood. To her Lady Macbeth she brought the wiles and seductiveness of a Cleopatra, so characteristic of her Sardou heroines. The purists argued that this was an unpalatable and unacceptable betrayal of dramatic convention. Tradition had dictated that Lady Macbeth should either be played as a queen who is stern and devoid of remorse or as a woman whose actions are motivated solely by love for her husband.[4] In the late eighteenth century, Mrs Siddons had established the fiendish Lady Macbeth, whereas Victorian criticism had predictably shown more interest in the latter – shortly to be epitomised by Ellen Terry's performance as the tragedy queen in 1888. Sarah's unconventional interpretation united love and ambition in a driving sexual force:

> Emphatically an actress of the day, she depicts for the present generation the kind of woman in whom alone apparently it is strongly interested, the dangerous siren-like creature by whose fascinations men are enslaved. In depicting Lady Macbeth as a being of this type, Mdme. Bernhardt runs counter to much recent criticism, the aim of which has been to represent Lady Macbeth as a woman endowed with most of the gentler and feminine virtues, the possession of which is balanced by a little over-anxiety for her husband's advancement. This Delilah-like character now assigned Lady Macbeth has, at least, the merit of being comprehensible. By women of this class the strongest natures of love have been subjugated. It is very easy to understand that Macbeth in the toils of such a one should prove weak and plastic. Anything rather than angelic or domestic is the being by whom he is stung into action.[5]

There is little doubt that the *femme fatale* figure was of paramount interest to Victorian audiences, as reactions to Bernhardt's repertoire had demonstrated. But in *Macbeth* it contradicted the preferred reading of the tragic hero; an emasculated Macbeth ran contrary to the Aristotelian notion of the flawed hero carried away by his 'vaulting ambition'. The majority of critics were not prepared to concede the merits of such a radical departure, especially as it erred dangerously in the direction of Sardou's formula: seduction given preference to the politics of good government. Four years later, when Ellen Terry substituted womanliness for the fiendish virago, Irving as Macbeth balanced the forces of virtue with evil ambition. But M. Marais (as the Samson to Bernhardt's Delilah) was seduced by passion rather than ambition and consequently upset the equilibrium of the tragic hero–heroine partnership. This gender-based reversal, which met with such critical hostility, indicated the power of Sarah's own sexual *femme fatale* image to subvert the classic discourse of the Shakespearean text.

Just as the shadow of Rachel fell across subsequent interpretations of Phèdre, so actresses undertaking Lady Macbeth were always haunted by the ghost of Mrs Siddons. Reference to the performances of the eighteenth-century tragedienne in the role was used to decry Sarah's use of pantomimic gesture in Shakespearean tragedy:

> Of Mrs. Siddons in this character it has been said by a famous critic that 'power was seated on her brow', that 'passion emanated from her breast as from a shrine', that she was 'tragedy personified'. Madame Bernhardt's power is rather seated in her arms and lungs. When she rushes up the steps to smear the faces of the grooms with blood it is with gesticulations, cries, and movements that indicate rather a violent effect to be resolute than the possession of a deep-seated and remorseless purpose.[6]

In the opinion of the *Era*, neither of the two great actresses succeeded in the banquet scene because both failed to reach the necessary note of tragic dignity. Sarah apparently copied her predecessor's mistake of dismissing her guests with a 'partez, partez' which 'was highly suggestive of the petty vexation of a modern hostess whose dinner party has been spoiled by an accident to the ice-pudding'.[7] The reviewer's rationale for why Sarah should adopt this tone is more interesting than the criticism *per se*. He attributes it to her attempt to make the tragedy queen more natural, an effect perceived as 'vulgar and commonplace', which reinforces the critical view of there being only one style suited to the genre of tragedy. As a result, Bernhardt's histrionic style – governed by emotional energy – was considered entirely inappropriate. Albeit spasmodically, her method of acting did occasionally manage to startle the audience into seeing a scene anew, notably in the sleepwalking sequence which was played as the antithesis to the troubled somnambulance of Mrs Siddons:

The sleep-walking scene was treated in a very unconventional fashion. No attempt was made to preserve the tragic solemnity hitherto assigned it. No fierce whisper denoted the inward struggle; light cries of pain and terror and a palpitating restlessness of affright were the chief means of suggesting underlying emotion. In place of the prolonged struggle to drag to her couch a cowed and conscience-stricken man, Mdme. Bernhardt went off with a run and a suppressed shriek. So different is this from anything that has before been seen, that its effect is startling.[8]

Far less effective were the moments in which traits of the French Classical style intruded. As English audiences were unaccustomed to the art of declamation, the reading of Macbeth's letter (which took the form of a Racinian tirade) seemed incongruous in Shakespeare. Similarly, the loud and passionate tones of Marais's Macbeth would probably have gone down well with French audiences whereas, given the traditions of English theatre, they were received as overdone, melodramatic and wanting in tragic dignity. Overall, the criticisms of the *Macbeth* production are interesting because they illuminate cultural and theatrical difference. Examining the reception of the production reveals as much about views on Shakespeare in performance as it does about Sarah's art. Evidently it was more acceptable for Bernhardt to appear before a London audience in a Racinian tragedy, in which histrionics, tirades and pantomimic gestures were received as conventions of the French stage (however inappropriate Sarah's style may have appeared to many of her own native critics and, indeed, to a few of her English reviewers), than to have them clashing discordantly with a Shakespearean discourse.

Early in 1886 Sarah appeared in her next Shakespearean tragedy when she played Ophelia in a production of *Hamlet* which opened at the Porte Saint-Martin on 27 February. Translated into alexandrines by two young members of her company (Louis Cressonnois and Charles Samson) this version of *Hamlet* was by all accounts even worse than Richepin's *Macbeth* and proved to be yet another of Sarah's ill-advised and ill-conceived productions.[9] Sarah had intended to include it in the London summer season that year, but it was hastily dropped at the last minute on the grounds of rehearsal strain. The hurried decision to exclude it from the London programme was a wise one given its apparent mediocrity.

Not until 1892 did Sarah offer her English audiences another tragedy queen from the Shakespearean repertoire, when she appeared before them as the seductive Cleopatra. The text was supplied by Sardou in collaboration with Emile Moreau, and was an adaptation rather than a translation of *Antony and Cleopatra*. The problem of hero–heroine centrality, which had plagued the *Macbeth* production, was resolved in this instance by Sardou's re-writing of Shakespeare, in which *Antony and Cleopatra* became *Cléopâtre*. Roman politics gave way to the Egyptian queen, or rather courtesan, for there is little majesty about Sardou's Cléopâtre. The collision of power, politics and passion is surrendered in favour of a *demi-monde* love-triangle in which an adulterous husband fails to give up his mistress.

When the play was premièred at the Porte Saint-Martin on 23 October 1890, it was only marginally successful. Marvellous scenery, captivating music by Xavier Leroux and a grand death scene were not enough to weave together the threads of an exotic patchwork of scenes through which an exceptionally languorous (if not bored) Bernhardt waded at her leisure, only occasionally rising to the magnetism of which she was capable. Nevertheless, the production was included in the repertoire for her global tour which began in January 1891 and lasted until November 1893, whereupon Sarah returned more permanently to Paris to take up the management of the Renaissance.

The play opened in London at the English Opera House on 28 May 1892 to a greater enthusiasm than Paris had shown. Audiences were delighted to have Sarah back in London (especially as the tour had kept her away in 1891), so delighted, in fact, that the criticisms were not as cutting as they might have been under normal circumstances. Because of her absence the previous year, Sarah's season was longer than usual and lasted for eight weeks instead of the usual two or four. Due to popular demand, the first fortnight was devoted entirely to performances of *Cléopâtre*.

Although there were some exclamations of horror over Sardou's treatment of Shakespeare, generally the play was read as a Sardou rather than a Shakespeare text. Given the disparity between the two, there was little point in engaging in a comparative

79

study. *Cléopâtre* was accepted for what it was, rather than criticised for what it might or should have been. Unlike the erudite debates over her unconventional Lady Macbeth, in this instance there was little discussion of character conception. Quite simply, Sarah was Cléopâtre. As two legendary figures, past and present, fused into one archetypal image of the *femme fatale*, Sarah had only to be herself. Previously, allusions to the Egyptian queen had informed both the descriptions of her stage heroines and of Bernhardt herself; now they were explicitly realised in this Eastern portrait of female sexuality. Current academic debate over whether Cleopatra had in fact been more Greek than Asiatic was of no interest to audiences, and historical accuracy (as regards her lusting after men for their power and not for their passion) was equally irrelevant.[10] The spectator's sole interest lay in Sarah's own creative vision of the Queen of the Nile.

Sarah's indifference to the production of the play in Paris was not repeated in London; visible traces of boredom were no longer in evidence:

> The great actress – greatest by far of her time – loves a London audience. She may be careless, indifferent, wilful, or mutinous else-where – seldom here, and never on a first night. It is an historical fact that the 'divine Sarah' never plays so well as on a first night in London. The sympathy she evokes is never lost on the artist, she feels by instinct that she is surrounded by a warm wave of appreciation.[11]

Another glittering and brilliant first night audience gave her an enthusiastic welcome. For her part, Sarah engaged all her seductive powers to sustain their attention throughout the long performance, which began at eight and lasted until midnight:

> On she came, with her heavy coils of Titian red hair; with her half-parted lips and winning smile; with her languorous movements; with her gorgeous garments and jewelled hands; with her soft raiments and blue eyes and bluer turquoises, and surrounded by sensuous magic of the East, in purple barges, on luxurious cushions, under feathered canopies, in the burning heat, in the cool night, this won-derful woman began to sing.[12]

The 'golden voice' seduced her lover and audience alike, as did her acting of the Sardou queen, a part which contained every conceivable situation for realising her superlative passionate temperament. Indeed, she was so suited to the role that she overcame the protraction of the piece and the inadequate patchwork script and proved herself more than equal to its arduous demands:

> To say so is to assert that the greatest living actress was at her best on Saturday night. It did not matter at all what phase she had to show of the character; it was represented wonderfully: her cunning, catlike wooing at first, her reckless abandon to voluptuous happiness, her vulgar, vile jealousy when she hears of Antony's marriage – were all triumphant. Last time she was here her voice seemed worn and wearied, but that was only temporary, for on Saturday night it was as wonderful as ever. Nothing seemed lacking of the dreamy murmuring music that seems more song than speech, and nothing of the horrible gutter screams of rage.[13]

To her beguiling vocal deliveries, Sarah brought a variety of snake-like body movements with which to pursue her lover. When seized by a fit of jealousy, she coiled ready to spring into an energetic and emotional outburst; when swayed by passion, her body undulated seductively across the stage in ruthless and physical pursuit of her lover. The sexual chess game played between the lovers – in which Antony was a mere pawn – suggested, as one reviewer put it, 'ideas' which it was 'hardly decorous to put into print'.[14] Though prudishly reluctant to be forthright, this statement hints at the overt sexuality of Sarah's performance as the key to the prurient fascination of the audience. A Victorian public could happily deceive itself into thinking that it went to the theatre out of the purest of motives: to see a great artist in an adaptation of a classic text. In reality it went with the craving of a sexually repressed society to see an actress who, with all her charms, subverted the Victorian ideology of passive femininity, of the sexless female. It was virtually impossible for an English actress to achieve the same image with impunity, because it was Sarah's 'Frenchness' or her Parisian aura which distanced her sufficiently in the eyes of the puritan from the notion of chaste and virginal womanhood.

By shifting the emphasis entirely on to Cléopâtre, Antony (played by M. Albert Darmont whose splendid physique rendered him a victim worthy of Cléopâtre's designs) was quite obscured in the action and was seen as rather ignoble in his domestic arrangements. The redistribution of sympathy and the realignment of culpability in Sardou's version worked wholely in Cléopâtre's favour. In any event, Bernhardt's consummate talent for death scenes was guaranteed to bring the curtain down on a note of queenly redemption. The art of blending sympathy and seduction, sin and saintliness, is indeed a fine one. In order to be convincing it must, as the success of *La Dame aux Camélias* or alternatively the failure of *Spiritisme* illustrate, embody the paradox of a passion which is essentially chaste. In the case of *Cléopâtre*, redemption is achieved by the absolute nature of the woman's passion; she has no interest in political gain. This explains to a large degree why *Cléopâtre* succeeded where *Macbeth* failed. Love in a power game is seen as sinful, but love for its own sake has the power of redemption.

Persecution of the heroine was another possible means for exacting pathos, and Sarah explored this avenue in two new roles which accompanied *Cléopâtre* in her lengthy London season: *Pauline Blanchard* and *Léah*. But neither of these were particularly successful. *Pauline Blanchard*, played only twice during the season (16 and 17 June), is an adaptation of the novel by Jules Case, and *Léah*, also given few performances, was based on Mosenthal's *Deborah*. Both were adapted by Sarah's young Antony, M. Albert Darmont (the former in collaboration with M. Humblot), and their failure was due largely to their inept skills as dramatists.

Pauline is a heroine who finds herself coerced into a hateful marriage and laments over the lover she has been forced to surrender. Unable to face life without her amour, she murders her husband. Inadequacies of composition (notably the absence of the heroine for much of the action prior to the final act) detracted from what might have been a thrilling Sardou-type climax. As the scene is set in rural Brittany, the heroine is of humble peasant origins, and these failed to match either the scale of her tragic dilemma or the violence of her emotions. Neither did Sarah's attempt to invest the heroine with a Keats-like, dreamy Arthurian aura, blend happily with her surrounds.

Léah, the persecuted Jewess, had previously been performed by Ristori and Kate Bateman (daughter of H.L. Bateman, the

82

American impresario who managed the Lyceum in the 1870s), and both performances were well-remembered. Yet when Sarah undertook the role, she was unable to raise either interest or sympathy. Darmont's conception of Léah was remarked upon as noticeably unsympathetic, and the passionate entreaties of Sarah, so suited to her Cléopâtre, jarred with the portrayal of the persecuted Jewish heroine, who needed a more refined and spiritual note in her proclamations of love for the God of Israel than did Cléopâtre in her passionate and physical advances towards Antony. Darmont took the role of Nathan the persecutor and matched his bad writing with equally poor acting. Matters were not helped by the stage-hand who interrupted a moving and theatrical moment in the third act by bringing the curtain down by mistake!

One of the key problems with *Léah* was its treatment of spiritual rather than physical love. On the one hand, while it was true that roles which erred in favour of the sinner rather than the saint were less likely to be successful, it was equally true on the other that saintliness without sin was limited in its appeal. Despite these drawbacks, Sarah was greatly interested in spiritual and mystical matters and could not resist the picturesque appeal of a zealous and virginal heroine. In particular she was drawn towards the saintly French heroine, Jeanne d'Arc.

Sarah brought the French maid to England two summers before her Cléopâtre, having first developed the character at the Porte Saint-Martin (3 January 1890). Her theatrical instincts lighted upon the appeal of Jeanne's legendary and patriotic image, which in itself could not fail to please her French audiences. However, she risked the potentially disastrous conflict of Jeanne's man-like and virginal qualities with her own exotic and sexual appeal. At least the respectable young French women, who agonised over whether they could permit themselves the pleasure of some of her less chaste heroines, could in this instance attend without fear of perjuring their souls.[15]

The play enjoyed only a moderate run lasting until mid-April, but it cost Sarah dearly in terms of her health. In the first act, as Jeanne appeals to God to be left in humble obscurity, Sarah reinforced the plea with a kneeling posture of supplication. The constant effort of going down on both knees resulted in an injury to one of them which was to keep her off the stage for two months.[16] When Sarah had recovered sufficiently, the play was brought to London in June 1890 to open at Her Majesty's Theatre. She played it on consecutive evenings (Sundays excluded) from 23 June to 5 July, and then offered a final week of plays containing single performances of *Adrienne Lecouvreur* and *La Dame aux Camélias*, followed by a final four nights of *La Tosca*.

Because of her injury, Sarah had to modify certain of her gestures, and even with the changes, it was obvious that she was still in poor health: 'those who recall the early performances see with regret that illness and mischance have compelled her to forego some of her previous business. In the first act, especially, the standing posture is assumed in place of the kneeling. Other signs of great suffering are also perceptible'.[17] After her first night as Jeanne, it was reported that she had returned to the Savoy Hotel and being unable to sleep had mistakenly taken an overdose of chloral.[18] Although Sarah was attended by a doctor from the French embassy and pronounced out of danger, on 27 June she collapsed during a performance of *Jeanne d'Arc*, which had to be abandoned. It was obvious that the actress was far from well during this season, and her acting throughout showed visible signs of strain.

Although the English public showed their customary warm applause for Sarah, they were far from delighted with either the play or its heroine. Like the Sardou plays, it was staged on a grand scale and paid particular attention to visual detail. It consisted of six tableaux: the 'voices', the conversion of the Dauphin, the armies on the banks of the Loire, the coronation of Charles VII, the prison and, finally, the stake. The English audiences did not share the French enthusiasm for the play's patriotic tirades, and neither could the poetical and picturesque qualities of the piece disguise its obviously inadequate and monotonous composition. Moreover, the divinely inspired heroine has little opportunity for striking out on her own, and flashes of the passionate and energetic Bernhardt were few and far between:

Perhaps the most striking moments in her performance are the close of the first tableaux, where Jeanne yields to the will of Heaven, and leaves her home, and the climax of the prison scene, when the captive maid mocks at and insults her conqueror, Warwick. But, taken as a whole, the part will never be cited as one in which the actress was able to exhibit her full powers, and we question whether any of her English admirers will care to witness for a second time a play which affords her so few dramatic chances.[19]

The question of why Sarah had not commissioned a new version of the Jeanne d'Arc legend was also raised, since the Jules Barbier text she used had originally been written for the actress Lia Félix in 1873 and was now rather dated in style. In the final phase of her career, Bernhardt achieved more success with Emile Moreau's *Le Procès de Jeanne d'Arc* (25 November 1909), though much of this was due to the thrill of seeing Bernhardt – by then in her mid-sixties – play the young maid. She certainly might have had better success with Joan in 1890 if Sardou's collaborator had been engaged to offer a better scripted version of the legend.

Despite all the various shortcomings of the 1890 *Jeanne d'Arc*, there was one aspect of the production which merited attention: its operatic quality. Interwoven with Barbier's text was the beautiful music of Charles Gounod. Reviewers, in turn, comment upon the musical quality of Sarah's voice, likening the combination of speech and music to the 'new-fashioned pianoforte reciters who add music to poetry'.[20] Sarah gave such recitals herself. In the 1897 season, which witnessed the failure of *Spiritisme*, for example, Sarah by contrast proved herself to be a successful attraction at a piano recital at St James's Hall. With musical accompaniment she recited 'Le Coucher de la Morte' by Count R. Montesquiou, the effect of which 'was almost that of "intonation", and mingled with, instead of standing out from that of the accompaniment'.[21] Such examples serve to indicate that Sarah's vision of the theatre aspired to the notion of an *opéra parlé*, approaching the Wagnerian fusion of the arts.[22] The pictorial quality of so many of her productions (notably the Sardou plays), the use of incidental music, the panoramic scale of action and the large groupings of performers would all seem to point in this direction.

In the case of *Jeanne d'Arc*, had the programme been shorter and the play more tightly constructed, perhaps Sarah's dreams of an *opéra parlé* might have met with a better reception and greater understanding. As it was, the final curtain fell on a sadly depleted audience, many· of whom had left well before the fiery martyrdom, which did not take place until a quarter past midnight. Even Sarah, as she uttered a last prayer amidst the choking fumes, had had enough. As the vision of saintliness lived her final moments, she was heard to utter a last request to the prompter for the 'Rideau! Rideau!'.[23]

*Jeanne d'Arc* and *Léah* had proved that saintliness alone lacked dramatic impact. Nevertheless, Bernhardt's early passion for religion continued to resurface in several of her dramatic choices, as she sought to deploy religious fervour in other tableaux. She had far more success with *Izéyl* by Armand Silvestre and Eugène Morand (Renaissance, 24 January 1894) in which spiritual concerns were combined with those of the flesh. In brief, *Izéyl* offers another version of the Christ and Magdalen story but transposes it to the East in the shape of Prince Kakyamouri-Goutama and the courtesan Izéyl. As the prince abdicates to become the founder of Buddhism, his younger brother Scyndia takes his place. Scyndia is in love with Izéyl. His mother the Princess Harastri, not knowing of her son's love for the courtesan, treats her with contempt, whereupon Izéyl, by way of revenge, sets out to seduce Kakyamouri. Ironically, it is she who is converted to Buddhism and who repents of her ways. Unaware of her conversion, Scyndia comes lusting after her, and in self-defence Izéyl kills him, for which act she in turn is condemned to death.

The play was chosen to open Sarah's London season at Daly's on 23 June 1894. For English audiences it had the popular appeal of a Sardou drama: passion, seduction, violence and martyrdom. Like Sardou's productions, its staging was designed on a grand scale, involving large groupings of actors all of whom revolved around the unifying presence of Sarah. In fact, the imprint of Sardou was so clearly stamped on this production that at least one critic attributed it to his authorship, rather than to that of Silvestre and Morand.[24] In particular, the killing of Scyndia was highly reminiscent of the stabbing in *La Tosca*, and the death scene, as Izéyl lingered long and lovingly in the arms of Kakyamouri, was calculated to a familiar lachrymal effect. It was a tribute to Sarah's talent that, as a fifty-year-old woman, she could still seduce and charm without fear of appearing grotesque or ridiculous. Both bodily and facially she retained a youthful vigour, and her voice, though strained at times, kept its golden tones.

The success of using the repentant courtesan-figure can be measured against the failure of a second London première offered in the middle week of Sarah's three-week 1894 season, *Les Rois* by Jules Lemaître. Lemaître was better known as a drama critic, and after seeing his play, there were many who suggested that he would do better to stick to his journalism and leave playwrighting well alone. *Les Rois* depicts a would-be socialist Prince Hermann, who is shot by his Princess when discovered in the embrace of his nihilist associate Frida. As Princess Wilhelmine, Sarah appeared relatively briefly, and while the shooting offered a fleeting opportunity for a display of jealousy and anger, this was poor compensation for having to sit through a sprawling, monotonous, ill-conceived and dramatically uninteresting plot. The play had not succeeded in Paris and was a poor choice of drama for inaugurating Sarah's management at the Renaissance (6 November 1893) for which it was rashly chosen. Whether Sarah had hoped to draw in the crowds because of the play's blatant parallel with the death of the Austrian Crown Prince Rodolphe and Baroness Veczera in 1889, or whether she had adopted the play as an attempt to engage in a more literary and less popular genre, is not clear. What is certain is that Sarah had to revive *Phèdre* in order to offset the disastrous beginnings of the Renaissance management, so why she should have taken it to London at all is a mystery. It was given only two performances (2 and 3 July) and was supported on either side by the popular favourites *La Dame aux Camélias* and *Fédora*.

Sarah's concern to engage in a more literary and less commercial dramatic output was unambiguously clear in her adoption of another lifelong writer–performer liaison with the verse dramatist Edmond Rostand. In April 1895 she created Rostand's Mélissinde in *La Princesse lointaine* at the Renaissance Theatre. *La Princesse lointaine* simply transposed the fairy-tale East of *Izéyl* to the distant shores of twelfth-century Tripoli in the age of the crusades and troubadours. Mélissinde is the love-quest of the legendary Joffroy Rudel, who crosses the seas with his troubador Bertrand, to find the princess who is renowned for her beauty.

Rostand supplemented the legend with a love interest between Bertrand and the princess, while Rudel is fatally ill and must rely on the troubador to do his courting for him. Though Mélissinde falls in love with Bertrand, believing him to be Rudel, she repents of her passion, rushes to the bedside of the dying prince and packs Bertrand off to the crusades.

Sarah included the play in the London summer season of 1895. Graceful, charming, picturesque and poetical though *La Princesse lointaine* was, the English critics considered that it was a weak alexandrine verse composition of little substance. Furthermore, the discourse of Sarah's modern woman, unhappily in love, clashed with the fairy-tale tenor of the piece. By adding the love interest between the princess and Bertrand to the dramatic action, Rostand had created an opportunity for passion and seduction à la Sardou but had failed to consider the inclusion of this motif within the overall lyrical spirit of the piece:

> A less happy thought was that of making Bertrand, when he is sent with the dying poet's missive, fall in love himself with the Princess, who reciprocates his passion. The episode it is true furnishes Mme Sarah Bernhardt with abundant opportunities for those caresses and blandishments, those outbursts of fierce passion and those melodious sustained elocutionary effects which appear to be regarded, alike by the actress and her patrons as indispensable to every new part she undertakes.[25]

All three plays – *Izéyl*, *Les Rois* and *La Princesse lointaine* – attempt, in their several ways, to combine literary aspirations with Bernhardt's skill as a performer and her stage image. *Les Rois*, as the least successful of these, failed because the central interest was political rather than romantic, because Sarah's role was peripheral rather than central to the action and, ultimately, because the rage of the jealous queen was a poor substitute for the impossible love of the 'chaste' courtesan. Both *Izéyl* and *La Princesse lointaine* recognise the centrality of the love-quest, though opt for a spiritual rather than physical union, which stopped short of the preferred realisation of a love which was both archetypally romantic and overtly sexual. The chivalric love-object quest encoded in these two performances was largely influenced by Sarah's interest in the poetry and painting of the

Pre-Raphaelite movement.[26] In Bernhardt's publicity photographs for *La Princesse lointaine*, the flowing mass of garlanded hair, the far-away gaze and the milky-white skin of the loosely draped figure were all redolent of a Pre-Raphaelite heroine.[27] From an academic point of view, the French critics were more interested in and understandably more appreciative of the verse composition of *La Princesse lointaine* than were their English counterparts. Perhaps in dismissing the play, English critics were overlooking the lyrical quality of Sarah's delivery. May Agate, an English actress tutored by Bernhardt, pays tribute to Sarah's 'lyrical genius' in her retrospective account *Madame Sarah*, wherein she recalls Sarah's rendition of Mélissinde, given during her teaching at the *cours*:

> It gave full scope to her lyrical genius and I shall never forget the oriental splendour she infused into the following lines:
>
> > 'Manteau brodé, stellé, gemmé, toi m'écrases
> > De corindons, de calcédoines, d' idocrases,
> > De jaspes, de béryls, de grenats syriens,
> > De tous ces vains cailloux, de tous ces riches riens,
> > Manteau, fardeau, sous qui je ploie et deviens blême,
> > O somptueux manteau, tu me sembles l'emblème
> > D'un autre que je porte et qu'on ne peut pas voir
> > Et qui me pèse encore, quand je t'ai laissé choir!'
>
> The semi-precious stones enumerated above became precious indeed as their rich and varied names fell from her lips. The very air seemed charged with their weight, and for the casting of the mantle she found an eloquent gesture of release which she then followed up with a much lighter, 'Prends mes perles aussi, tout ce qui me déguise', but only at the 'Ouf! Me voici coiffée à peu près à ma guise', did you feel a cooling breeze sweep across the stage.[28]

It was probably asking too much of English audiences to take in all these points of instruction relating to the delivery of French verse. For this reason the narrative quality of Sardou's pictorially based dramas was more readily accessible and decodable. Although Sarah's gift for verse speaking was overlooked, one would not wish on the other hand to overstate the case for Rostand's first Bernhardt play. The dramatist's son, Maurice Rostand, attempts an over-zealous defence of his father's play when he balances the immediate popularity of the Sardou plays against theatrical history, which has been, he argues, kinder to *La Princesse lointaine*.[29] The disparity between the two styles which Maurice wished to establish is an overstated claim and ignores the Sardou strategies encoded in the Rostand text, despite its lyrical gloss. Furthermore, it fails to credit the audience enthusiasm and excitement for the physical passions over the lyrical and spiritual union.

In Sarah's quest to find alternative writers to Sardou, she also accepted *Lysiane* by Romain Coolus, which emulated the strategy of *Gismonda* by attempting to combine passion and maternity. As such, *Lysiane* was a further attempt to create a role which took account of Bernhardt's maturing years. *Lysiane* reverses the theme of Augier's *L'Aventurière* and depicts the 'merry widow' (as opposed to the gulled widower) falling prey to a fortune-hunting profligate. Filial intervention saves Lysiane from disgrace, and though at first she resents this interference, she is ultimately guided by her maternal instincts towards reconciliation with her son.

The play was given a mere two performances in the two-week summer season of 1898, and critical reaction indicates that for most reviewers, this was two too many. Objections to the poor quality of the playwrighting aside, critics were not enamoured of a portrait of passion in an older woman. The occasional flashes of anger and passion in *Lysiane* – echoes of the younger Bernhardt heroines – were considered the best moments and indicate that this was the type of role in which audiences wished her to continue. An emphasis on mature womanhood seriously conflicted with their preferred image of archetypal passion and femininity. On the one hand, Sarah (as Lysiane) continued to highlight the seductive image which she had forged for herself by dressing in the customary clinging costumes identified, as biographer Reynaldo Hahn describes, by their 'coupe sarahbernhardtesque', spiraling about her body accentuating every seductive and serpentine movement.[30] On the other, the role itself failed to support this favoured image of everlasting youth and beauty. The timeless and eternal qualities of the one clashed with the mortal and maternal coding of the other. That Sarah was aware of these difficulties is shown by her attempts in maturing years to maintain a youthful stage image by means of an increasing recourse to cosmetic artifice and to find roles which would support the myth of Bernhardtesque youth, rather than emphasise the aging process.

Altogether, this long procession of tragedy queens, fairy-tale princesses, martyrs and repentant courtesans, in a variety of historical, distant, foreign and legendary settings, reveals the larger-than-life quality of the heroines Sarah chose to play. The roles in which she was most at home and most successful were those which afforded the paradoxical opportunity for 'chaste' passion. The dull virtue of Saint Joan or the sins of a Lady Macbeth polarised the roles of saint and sinner in a way which failed to interact with Sarah's own image: a conflation of the two extremes into the sexual but chaste allure of the 'saintly sinner'. She was seen at her best when the role and the image of the actress synthesised into a portrait of physical passion, paradoxically purged of sin through saintly redemption.

## Notes

1. See E. Pronier, *Sarah Bernhardt: Une vie au théâtre* (Geneva: Editions Alex. Julien, n.d.), p. 85.
2. *Era*, 12 July 1884.
3. *Daily Telegraph*, 5 July 1884.
4. For the debate over the two interpretations, see *Daily News*, 5 July 1884.
5. *Pall Mall Gazette*, 5 July 1884.
6. *Daily News*, 5 July 1884.
7. *Era*, 12 July 1884.
8. *Pall Mall Gazette*, 5 July 1884.
9. For details see Pronier, *Sarah Bernhardt*, p. 87.
10. See *Spectator*, 11 June 1892, for a discussion of Cleopatra's character.
11. *Daily Telegraph*, 30 May 1892.
12. Ibid.
13. *Pall Mall Gazette*, 30 May 1892.
14. Ibid.
15. Verneuil *La Vie merveilleuse de Sarah Bernhardt* (Montréal: Editions Variétés, 1942), p. 198, cites an article from *Le Gaulois*, November 1889, announcing the *Jeanne d'Arc* production, which makes specific reference to the women and girls who wanted to go and see Sarah

but were uncertain of her roles.

16. For details see Pronier, *Sarah Bernhardt*, p. 92.
17. *Morning Post*, 24 June 1890.
18. Reported in the *Pall Mall Gazette*, 24 June 1890.
19. *Pall Mall Gazette*, 25 June 1890.
20. *Daily Telegraph*, 24 June 1890.
21. *Daily Telegraph*, 7 July 1897.
22. Sarah coins the term *opéra parlé* herself in an interview about her production of *Médeé* by Catulle Mendès in *Revue d' Art dramatique*, November 1898, p. 318.
23. *Daily Telegraph*, 24 June 1890.
24. See Addison Bright's review in the *Theatre*, August 1894, pp. 83–5.
25. *Daily News*, 19 June 1895.
26. Pronier, *Sarah Bernhardt*, p. 232, cites the probability of her acquaintance with Edward Burne-Jones.
27. A selection of publicity photographs for the play is contained in William Emboden, *Sarah Bernhardt*, pp. 97–9.
28. May Agate, *Madame Sarah* (London: Home & Van Thal, 1945), p. 52.
29. Maurice Rostand, *Sarah Bernhardt* (Paris: Calmann Lévy, 1950), p. 48.
30. Reynaldo Hahn, *La Grande Sarah* (Paris: Hachette, 1929), pp. 48–9.

# 6 Stages in Rivalry

By the turn of the century Sarah's stage career had spanned over thirty years, and during two-thirds of this time, she had paid regular visits to London. Her seasons in the capital were a highly popular tradition and an almost annual event. During this period, however, other actresses and companies rivalled the French actress on the English stage. Sarah's own style of acting encouraged a number of imitators, though none of these seemed to match the Bernhardtesque fascination. A more serious threat to Sarah's stardom was posed by a younger generation of actresses experimenting with new styles. Sarah was conscious of the youthful competition but wisely did not abandon the image and legend she had fostered, merely continuing to exploit it, both on and off-stage. Her need to secure large incomes for her vast expenditures, and her consequent reliance on the commercialism of her theatre, constantly attracted the censorship of those critics who saw nothing in her art but a mannered style, self-advertisement and grand personality cult. Yet it was precisely this larger-than-life glamour and theatrical style which Sarah knew instinctively would keep her at the pinnacle of international stardom, despite the challenge of the 'new'.

In production reviews from the middle phase of Sarah's career, young playgoers new to theatre are urged to go and see Sarah while the opportunity is open to them. Implicit in this advocacy is not only Sarah's reputation as the finest living nineteenth-century exponent of the histrionic method, but also the notion that her method belongs firmly to the old century and not to the new, and is not to be in evidence much longer. The era of the international actress and the nineteenth-century star-system was rapidly drawing to a close in the wake of the new experimental theatre and the regeneration of drama in movements such as repertory theatre. This meant that the centrality of the star as manager and performer was gradually being eroded in favour of a collective ensemble performance style, which abandoned the long runs and tried, where possible, to place artistic considerations above

93

commercial interests. Such policies radically affected the style and status of the performer. By the turn of the century in England, for example, a new generation of actresses had been established. They came from the erudite, middle classes and, in the climate of the suffrage movement, were more politically aware than their predecessors. They populated the smaller theatres and pioneered the new drama by writers such as Ibsen, Shaw and Galsworthy. The style and aims of the new actress (Florence Farr, Janet Achurch, Elizabeth Robins et al.) were so remote from Bernhardt's, that it is futile to set up comparisons, as Bernard Shaw did, simply to herald the new at the expense of the old. Of more interest and value is a comparative view of the stars who occupied a high status in England or held an international place in the theatre, during the years of Sarah's English stage career, in order to see the influence of Sarah's style and to assess the contribution and contrast of younger rivals.

Although critics were always quick to chastise Sardou and his followers for their performer-based plays, it ought to be pointed out that, because of the structure and star-hierarchy of the theatre, both the writer and performer had little choice in the matter. Popular tastes dictated a star-based script in which the heroine passed through all the phases from love-beguiled to the martyrdom of an agonising death scene. The French theatrical canon of the nineteenth century had the richest supply of this popular, melodramatic, 'weepy' drama, and many international star-actresses drew heavily upon the French repertoire for their roles. For instance, on the eve of her Paris début in 1897, Eleonora Duse, Sarah's younger, Italian rival and rising star of the 1890s, was about to offer an entirely French repertoire in Italian translations before she was urged to find (with difficulty) some appropriate native dramas.[1] (This did not, however, prevent her from opening in *La Dame aux Camélias* on Sarah's own Renaissance stage, thereby heightening the sense of theatrical contest which arose whenever these two rivals performed in the vicinity of one another.)

One of the first of several actresses to establish herself in a French-based repertoire of Bernhardtesque drama was Mme Modjeska. Modjeska, a child of the Polish revolution, began her acting career on the Warsaw stage. Later, when she emigrated to

America, she was forced to master English in order to resume her career in the theatre. She achieved success in a performance of *Adrienne Lecouvreur* at San Francisco in 1877 and, with American accolades behind her, came to England where she first appeared in *Heartsease* in May 1880. As previously described, this modified version of Dumas's drama was not well adapted and restricted the actress's opportunity for passionate display. Yet both the play and Modjeska's style prompted critical cross-referencing between the Polish and the French actress, the latter appearing successfully for the first time with her own company.

In 1881 Modjeska was featured as the main attraction in a season of plays by Wilson Barrett at the Court Theatre, where she appeared both as Marguerite and Adrienne. In June, Wilson Barrett transferred his company to a larger venue – the Princess's Theatre – and Modjeska inaugurated the move by opening as the frivolous Froufrou in a translation by Comyns Carr. This meant that Sarah and Modjeska were playing the role at the same time. Modjeska was commended for her interpretation, even though she clearly failed to reach the heights of Sarah's dynamic passion. The larger venue was detrimental to her style which, unlike Sarah's, relied on subtle expression and the use of minimal rather than broad gesture. Like the French actress, she was more comfortable in the play's later serious scenes than in the gaiety of the opening tableaux. She always performed in English (something Sarah was never able to do), though she retained a slight accent which worked to her advantage, because it placed her wayward heroines as safely continental – rather than English – in origin. Because Sarah's performances coincided with Modjeska's, she was able to see the actress for herself and reported that she was greatly pleased by her method of acting, which showed 'both charm and vigour'.[2]

The traits of the Bernhardtesque in Modjeska's style were more clearly emphasised and encoded in the method of the English actress, Mrs Bernard-Beere. In her youth, Mrs Bernard-Beere had been a frequent visitor to the Comédie Française and had warmly admired the talent of Aimée Desclée. In her débuts at the Opéra Comique and St James's in the late 1870s, she proceeded to establish herself as an actress with potential and in May 1883 put her embryonic talent to the test, when she

95

appeared as the Russian princess Fedora in an English version staged by the Bancrofts at the Haymarket. As the critics were familiar with Sarah's Paris production of *Fédora*, destined for a London performance in July, they seriously doubted whether Mrs Bernard-Beere's interpretation could possibly match Sarah's success. Yet she surprised them all by her commanding picture of pathos and passion. Though the English version (by Mr Herman C. Merivale) had prudishly opted to have Fédora and Loris unambiguously united in marriage, the tragic outcome was consistent with the original, and Mrs Bernard-Beere triumphed with a memorable 'haunted look' in the tragedy of the last act. She was well supported in her endeavours by a strong company and by the Bancrofts' staging, which avoided the long and clumsy scene changes for which the French productions were notorious. Mrs Bernard-Beere's style was coloured by unmistakable Bernhardtesque traits, but it was also true that her interpretation was more than a careful study and imitation of the French actress:

> It will be conceded that Mrs. Bernard-Beere has made a very accurate and exhaustive study of Sarah Bernhardt's acting. Without such a study the success might not have been so great. But at the same time the success achieved is far more than that of imitation; it reveals a sudden and unexpected power in a young actress, and power is exactly the thing in which our cleverest and most promising actresses are lamentably deficient . . .[3]

In 1887, Mrs Bernard-Beere created the role of Lena Despard in *As in a Looking Glass* which Sarah did not play until two years later, when for once general practice was reversed, and reviewers had a native production for their blueprint. The play, an adaptation of the novel by F.C. Philips, was unusual because it treated the subject of passion, a topic almost exclusively monopolised by the French theatre in the last century. Briefly, the play relates the story of Lena, a fortune hunter who seeks out a man of means and then ironically begins to fall truly in love with him. As her love is awakened, so her real character is exposed, and she takes her own life before her husband has had a chance to utter words of forgiveness.

As Lena, Mrs Bernard-Beere revealed a maturity of method which owed much to Sarah's histrionic style. She had learnt to capture the essence of female distress and readily effected the reversal from designing huntress to a woman with a heart and conscience. À la Bernhardt, she incorporated the extensive use of facial and bodily gestures to externalise the inner turmoil of emotion. Her Bernhardtesque gestures were large and energetic in accordance with the magnitude of her dilemma. In particular she exploited the dramatic potential of the scenes of death and confession. It was probably these moments of dramatic impact and intensity which aroused Sarah's interest in the play and caused her to stage her own production.

Sarah's London production of *Léna* opened on 9 July 1889 and ran for the first week of a season that had been planned as five weeks but which was then cut back to four, after the cancellation of a week of *Théodora* performances. Sarah's health proved troublesome that summer and significantly marred the opening night of *Léna*. The start of the performance was subject to a long delay, until finally Berton came forward to beg the audience's indulgence and to explain Sarah's indisposition. The performance went ahead, although it was painfully obvious that Sarah was well below her usual standard. Performing with her in the role of the husband was an emaciated Damala who had rejoined Sarah for what was to be the final phase of his career and, moreover, of his life.

The French version was based on the English novel rather than on the play and was adapted by M. Berton and Mme Van de Velde. The critics held mixed views on the merits of the adaptation, particularly as Sarah's lack of brilliance on this occasion made its inadequacies all the more glaring. The quietness and restraint which characterised Sarah's performance in the opening scenes was probably the result of her indisposition rather than a conscious mode of interpretation, and critics refrained from a comparative analysis with the English production at this point, as Sarah offered so little on which to base a comparison. Eventually the patience and tolerance of the audience were rewarded by a superb death scene which surpassed all of her other tragic declines to date. For the wild agonies of Mrs Bernard-Beere's Lena, Sarah substituted a scene of unspoken and silent agony. It was an impressive tableau which was described repeatedly and in extensive detail in the reviews the next morning and made amends for much that had gone before:

Mrs. Bernard-Beere adopted a virulent poison of some sort, and skilfully harrowed the feelings of the public by her long-drawn-out spasms and convulsions. Madame Bernhardt's death is terribly impressive by its absolute freedom from conventional agony. Repudiated by her husband, whom she passionately loves . . . the French Lena, in a condition of blank despair, looks about for some means of ending her ruined life. Not a word is spoken; the scene from first to last is purely pantomime. Her eyes light upon a dagger; she takes it up, examines it, and throws it down with a shudder. From a cupboard she next obtains a bottle of chloral, pours a fatal draught into a glass, and hastily swallows it, with a slight gesture of disgust. Then she walks about the room and, discovering her husband's portrait on the mantelpiece, takes it down while the drug is visibly producing its effect upon her system. In a dazed condition she stumbles rather than falls upon a couch. Her husband is heard imploring admission to the locked apartment; she can hear his voice, but now she is powerless to respond. She can but clutch with her hands, so to speak, at the forgiveness he offers her, and when, having forced his way in, he rushes forward to clasp in his arms her inert form she falls upon the floor dead. None of Madame Bernhardt's famous death scenes equals this in intensity or thrilling effect; it is a marvellous *tour de force*.[4]

This detail is typical of the reviews which followed the opening night. The absence of speech and sole recourse to movement singled out this tableau of death from her previous death scenes. Although the English production was alluded to as finer overall in terms of staging and dramatic composition, Sarah had proved that one spark of her brilliance was enough to outshine her rival. Mrs Bernard-Beere, endowed with her Pre-Raphaelite, Magdalen-red hair and heralded as 'the English Sarah Bernhardt', did not surpass the French actress from whom she took her cue for her method and style. She did go on, however, to fulfil the prophecies of becoming a fine actress and to establish herself in roles as the woman with a past, notably when she played the lead in Oscar Wilde's *Woman of No Importance* in 1893.

In terms of dramatic representations of the erring and repentant woman, 1893 was a significant year as it witnessed the première of Pinero's *The Second Mrs Tanqueray* and brought overnight fame to the actress who played Paula Tanqueray, Mrs Patrick Campbell. Pat Campbell was an actress of erratic genius. As Paula she captured the spirit of the fallen woman who is cast out by respectable society and proved that an English play and performer could rival the French tradition of the saintly sinner, as established by Dumas et al. She went on to preach 'free love' as Agnes in Pinero's *The Notorious Mrs Ebbsmith* in March 1895 and two months later appeared as Fedora.

Her Russian princess was found wanting in the sensuality which had characterised Sarah's interpretation. For the first three acts she was remarkably restrained and moved through the action in a trance-like, dream-like state which revealed none of the role's emotional potential. Her underacting in the first three acts was redeemed in the fourth by a performance of 'a pathetic beauty, a natural charm, and a passionate tenderness such as have never yet been applied to this most difficult part by Sarah Bernhardt or any of her successors'.[5] In her youth, Mrs Campbell was endowed with an almost painful slenderness and possessed a physical charm and beauty which lent themselves to a portrait of delicate femininity. The wildness of her hair and the haunting gaze of her dark eyes against the pallor of a sculptured marble beauty conjured up an image of the ethereal fairy-tale princess, who is not of this world. The theatre critic William Archer thought that Sarah had indeed found a serious rival 'in the art of wearing clothes' and describes the vision Mrs Campbell created on her first entrance: 'her tall willowy figure divined around the ample folds of a flowing white garment'.[6] Yet as the vision moved and spoke, it failed to combine the image of fragile femininity with sensual gesture in the way that was so typical of Bernhardt's movement and voice. Mrs Campbell's less-than-graceful walk was supported by agitated gestures which at times seemed to be little more than fidgeting, and the note of vocal passion was betrayed by a tone of childish petulance. In short, she lacked the serpentine sexual wiles of the French Fédora. Had Mrs Campbell applied herself more thoroughly to the art of the theatre instead of adopting an all too frequently dilettante attitude and had she overcome the constraints of English womanliness in favour of continental self-abandon and sexuality, she may indeed have proved a serious rival for Sarah. Instead, she preferred to divide her erratic magnetism between the stage and the high-society circles of England and, later on in her career, America.

Among English actresses, Ellen Terry paralleled Sarah most

closely in terms of status and age. Yet in respect of style, the two could not have been more radically disparate. Ellen's career was devoted in the main to Shakespearean roles. This was because her repertoire was largely governed by her partnership with Henry Irving at the Lyceum, which began about six months before Sarah's London début and lasted for over twenty years. Ellen continually found herself having to fall in with Irving's wishes and artistic choices, and the majority of their productions were chosen to suit his talents rather than hers. Her ardent wish, for example, to play Rosalind in *As You Like It* was never fulfilled because Irving disliked the lesser role of Orlando. Ellen's temperament, however, seemed suited to the security, partnership and friendship which her association with Irving offered. But Sarah was far too high-spirited and independent to place herself in a position of constant professional subjugation. Her various liaisons with playwrights and actors had lead to some appalling dramatic choices and poor productions, but no one man permanently dictated her artistic programme, winning for her an independence which made her actress–manager status all the more formidable in terms of sexuality and power. Where Sarah's image denoted overt sexuality and seductive femininity, Ellen's was one of respectable English womanliness, despite the fact that she was the mother of two illegitimate children. The two actresses held a mutual respect for each other's work. Ellen was a glowing admirer of the French actress. She was rather in awe of Sarah's lack of respect for convention and was more than a little envious of her independence, as is revealed in her description of the supper organised for her and Henry Irving's hundredth performance of *Romeo and Juliet* in 1882:

> At the supper on the stage after the hundredth performance, Sarah Bernhardt was present. She said nice things to me, and I was enraptured that my 'vraies larmes' should have pleased and astonished her! I noticed that she hardly ever moved, yet all the time she gave the impression of swift, butterfly movement. While talking to Henry she took some red stuff out of her bag and rubbed it on her lips! This frank 'making-up' in public was a far more astonishing thing in the 'eighties than it would be now. But I liked Miss Sarah for it, as I liked her for everything.[7]

She goes on to praise Sarah's 'exotic' quality and her abilities as a manager, declaring her to be the 'equal of any man' in this respect. Clearly, Sarah's policy of leasing Parisian theatres at different stages of her career enabled her to develop her own directorial aspirations, whereas Ellen always had to defer to Irving on matters of stage-craft. Ellen further recalls her delight over Sarah's performances in *Cléopâtre*, *La Dame aux Camélias* and *Froufrou*. Once she had seen Sarah in the latter, Ellen rather regretted her own performances as Froufrou which she had given during a provincial tour in the early 1880s. In a self-critique, Ellen identifies her main deficiency in the role as a lack of 'pace', attributed in part to language (because 'English cannot be phrased as rapidly as French'), but she also notes that foreign actors performing in English do so with a greater 'rapidity' than the native speaker.[8] She might also have added to this the disparate ideologies of English and continental femininity: the idyllic, spiritual and passive versus the voluptuous, seductive and sexual, the reserved and languorous mood of the first contrasting starkly with the energetic and dynamic mode of the second.

Although Sarah was indisputably the most popular French actress to appear in the seasons organised by Mayer and Hollingshead, there were other French actresses who aroused considerable interest. During the 1880s Jane Hading, Sarah's rival who managed to lure Damala away to the Gymnase, was a notable favourite, and her performance in *Le Maître de Forges* was acclaimed in Paris and London. Her repertoire at the Gymnase identified her with the new social drama, and like Mrs Pat, she had a frail and feminine figure suited to the role of the *demi-monde* outcast. Yet Hading relied too heavily on technique and as a result failed to captivate her audience in the way that Bernhardt's histrionic method did. J.T. Grein, critic and pioneer of the Independent Theatre Society, analysed her limitations in a retrospective turn-of-the-century study, identifying her 'want of magnetism' as her failure to 'communicate to others what she was supposed to feel': 'she had reached a certain level and there she remained; always a distinguished, fascinating actress, but never great'.[9] Though with time she modified her use of technique in favour of the 'inner being', she could not, as Grein explained, make herself 'mistress' of the spectator's 'emotion'.[10]

In the London season of 1903 Bernhardt appeared in two roles which were specifically associated with Hading: the unfortunate heroine in Alphonse Daudet's *Sapho* and Joséphine de Beauharnais in *Plus que reine*. Neither of these were outstanding successes for Sarah. The *demi-monde* world of *Sapho* (first interpreted by Hading at the Gymnase in 1885) did not incite renewed interest, although the pathos and magnetism of Sarah's performance (precisely the qualities which Hading fell short of) were as spellbinding as ever. The Napoleonic play, *Plus que reine*, by M. Bergerat, which focuses on the divorce between Joséphine and Napoleon, offers little opportunity for emotional display. Whatever Hading had found in the role to suit her talents, it was obvious that the part was beneath Sarah's histrionic talent. The last act for example, in which Joséphine discovers that her secret access to Napoleon's bedroom has been blocked off, was pure melodrama – especially as Joséphine, after banging her head against the blocked passageway, reappeared 'with blotches of red paint on her face', the 'vulgarity' of which could only appeal 'to the butcher-boy in the gallery'.[11]

For a style which offered a slightly better balance between technique and emotion, one had to look to the French actress Julia Bartet, 'La Divine'. Sarah's abrupt exit from the Comédie Française had left a gap which was filled by the elegant and lady-like Bartet, who was as conciliatory as Bernhardt was rebellious. In terms of image, Bartet and Bernhardt were total opposites. Bartet epitomised the dignity and reverential status of the Comédie Française where she performed in both classical tragedy and in a modern repertoire of plays. Untouched by scandal and keeping her private life private, Bartet was as dignified and restrained, both on and off-stage, as Bernhardt was wilful, scandalous and piquantly exotic. Aside from her classical successes, chief among which was her interpretation of Bérénice, Bartet was particularly noted for her performances in certain of Dumas's dramas and at the turn of the century was instrumental in promoting the plays of one of the new dramatists, Paul Hervieu.

The role which first brought her public acclaim was as Dumas's heroine in *Denise* at the Comédie Française in 1885, a part which drew directly on her image of respectability and purity to overcome the play's risqué subject (the exposure of a profligate who ultimately agrees to marry the woman he has wronged). In January 1887 she created the Dumas heroine Francine de Rivorelles in *Francillon*, and the following summer Bernhardt appeared in London as this Bartet heroine. Reviews of the production took the form of a comparative analysis of styles, while little was said about the play itself, which was out of favour. It was unpopular both in terms of subject (the dramatisation of a debate over whether a wife is entitled to be as sexually promiscuous as her husband) and because of the verbosity of its composition. The plot, which turns on Francine's threat to follow her husband's example and to have an affair – a threat which is never actually carried out – was considered a sham. As the wife turns out to be of a truly chaste and virtuous disposition, the role was admirably suited to Bartet's stage image and style. Where she excelled was in her evocation of womanliness and purity. This side was totally missing from Bernhardt's interpretation, and though she proved she could invest her character with an appropriate aristocratic aura, her forte instead lay in her scenes of contemptuous tirades, delivered while she spiralled angrily over the wretch of a husband. The *Pall Mall Gazette* summarised the key differences in style as follows:

Mdme. Bernhardt's performance of Francine de Riverolles compares very favourably in all respects but one with that of Mdlle. Bartet, who created the part in Paris. Mdlle. Bartet was certainly more of the great lady. She dressed the part more quietly (Mdme. Bernhardt's toilette in the first act is surely extravagant), and she made us feel more vividly than Mdme. Bernhardt how foreign to her normal nature is the wild adventure of the masquerade at the restaurant. On the other hand, she was far less sympathetic and touching than Mdme. Bernhardt. Though rather mechanical in some scenes, and apt to hurry her delivery more than the nervous excitement of the character demands, the Francillon of last evening was in the main infinitely true and touching. The tenderness of her appealing womanhood was no less admirable than the vibrating intensity of her scorn, and the subdued agony of her humiliation. In short, there is a subtle and irresistible note of pathos in Mdme. Bernhardt's Francillon which Mdlle. Bartet entirely missed.[12]

The argument is similar to that used against Hading: Bartet's want of magnetism highlighted against the irresistible Bernhardtesque spell.

In Bartet's turn-of-the-century performances in Paul Hervieu's plays, which focused their debate largely on the position of women in society, the same womanly dignity was used to soften contentious arguments about the inequality of the sexes. On the occasion of Bartet's London performance in Hervieu's *Le Dédale* in 1908, Max Beerbohm attempted an overview of the two actresses. He describes Bartet as demonstrating an 'air of official reserve', of being an 'eminently "safe" actress', as someone who is conscious of 'having mastered thoroughly all that in the art of acting can be taught by the most distinguished school of acting in the world'.[13] Yet this is used to preface his main criticism of the actress, her emphasis on tradition at the expense of feeling: 'the method of expression has crushed whatever there was to be expressed'.[14] By contrast, in Sarah's method, whatever 'her eccentricities, her follies and vulgarities', there would also be 'flashes of truth and power – flashes of the true Sarah'.[15] This pinpoints the accomplishments of the one and the genius of the other.

The new-woman roles in Hervieu's plays held little attraction for Sarah, possibly because their smaller domestic settings did not present her with sufficient opportunity for the large pictorial vistas of passion which she preferred. She appeared in only two of his plays. In Paris and London in 1907, she played Thérèse in *Le Réveil* which was first performed by Bartet in 1905. As the wife and mother who nearly falls from grace but returns to the bosom of her family, Sarah was singularly insignificant, and there was little doubt among the English critics that the play was markedly unworthy of her talent. The only drama which Hervieu wrote specifically for Sarah was *Théroigne de Méricourt*, played at the Théâtre Sarah Bernhardt in 1902. As an historical drama set in the days of the French Revolution, it was Hervieu's one and only play on a large scale and involving a huge cast. Unfortunately, his skills as a playwright were not equal to the demands of the historical panorama, and the play failed to stimulate interest.

Although Hading and Bartet were both popular performers in London, in the view of the English critics neither were equal to Sarah's genius. In the younger French actress Gabrielle Réjane, however, Sarah found a more serious rival. With a Conservatoire training and apprenticeships at the Vaudeville and Variétés,

Réjane rose to Parisian fame as the working-class heroine in an adaptation of the Goncourts' novel, *Germinie Lacerteux* performed at the Odéon in 1888. During the 1880s she visited London, appearing only in supporting roles rather than in a star capacity, and started to make an impression on English audiences, notably as Baronne Doria in Sardou's *Odette*, playing along side Mdlle Blanche Pierson in the title role. In the summer of 1894, she gained the recognition of English audiences and critics when she appeared in Sardou's *Madame Sans-Gêne*, produced in Paris the previous year at the Vaudeville by her husband and manager, M. Porel. The huge Vaudeville success was repeated at the Gaiety Theatre 'and it was then first that London awoke to the fact that Paris boasted another great actress besides Madame Bernhardt'.[16]

The magnetism of Réjane was radically different to any other actress. She had neither the statuesque beauty nor feminine fragility of Bartet or Hading, nor the seductive charm of Bernhardt. Hers was an irregular beauty, epitomised by her curiously lopsided facial expression, captured in Aubrey Beardsley's portrait drawings. Although she played a variety of heroines, her early major successes — as Germinie and as the washerwoman-turned-aristocrat Cathérine in *Madame Sans Gêne* — encoded an enduring signification of the Parisian in her image. This was not the Parisian in the Bernhardt sense of passion and exotica, but Parisian as in the *peuple*.[17] She brought to her roles a sense of the Bohemian, the vulgarity of the *gamin*, the poverty and degradation of the Parisian gutter, rather than the seductive and licentious underworld of the *demi-monde*. She did not glamorise or idealise her heroines to achieve an electrifying effect, as Bernhardt did, but brought out the beast in the beauty.

Réjane established a vast repertoire of victim–heroine roles. In 1897 she brought Maurice Donnay's *La Douleureuse* to her London season at the Lyric and argued Donnay's case for equality between the sexes in affairs of the heart, not by means of a sculptured or seductive pathos, but by evoking a Bohemian spirit of suffering in which a sense of the comic and tragic collided. Her London season coincided with Bernhardt's, and comparisons, or rather contrasts, were immediately invited when they both appeared as Gilberte in *Froufrou*. Kate Terry Gielgud points towards an important difference between the two, when she

105

distinguishes Sarah's Gilberte as an identifiable type on a 'grandiose scale' and cites Réjane's Froufrou as a means to show the character in progress, to account for the way her family and social environment have moulded her.[18] Sarah's victim–heroine 'type' relied on the unquestioned transformation from sinner to saint; the shades of Réjane's study answered the question of why Gilberte acts as she does.

This marks a radical change in acting styles. Réjane did not disguise the workings of her heroine with a histrionic veneer. She was not afraid to be ugly or to expose the ugliness society creates (an approach which notably characterised her 1901 London performance in the role of Sapho, in which she was more successful than either Bernhardt or Hading). In many ways, Réjane bridges the gap between the star-system and the rise of the naturalist school of writers and performers. The roles she undertook were still those of the star–victim–heroine, but they aimed to emphasise the reason for her plight, rather than to concentrate solely on the heroic pathos of martyrdom. As the naturalist drama showed the social construction of the victim–heroine and did not attempt to disguise the ugliness and sordid aspects of life, beauty was no longer a prerequisite. The heroine needed to reflect the beast in the society which had made her. Where, in time, some English critics showed a preference for Réjane over Bernhardt, their choice needs to be contextualised as the welcoming of a new style, a different concept of theatre responding to the growing contemporaneous interest in the interaction of society and the individual.

During 1893 when Sarah was absent from London on a global tour, Eleonora Duse made a brilliant English début in an Italian version of *La Dame aux Camélias* with a performance which initiated a flow of comparative criticism which lasted for years. The two Marguerites had little in common, except for the shared spirit of dramatic genius. Sarah's histrionic method centred on the realisation of the brilliant, painted courtesan–beauty of the *demi-monde*. The Italian Marguerite, unadorned and unpainted, incarnated the spirit of 'truth' rather than 'beauty' and demonstrated with simplicity and naturalness the woman in love:

Sarah is a complex artificial product, a strange, exotic, orchidaceous

# God's Message to All

## The Gospel - God's provision for your Salvation

"I want to remind you of the gospel...by this gospel you are saved...:that CHRIST DIED for our sins according to the Scriptures, that HE WAS BURIED, that HE WAS RAISED on the third day according to the Scriptures." *I Corinthians 15:1-4*

"We all, like sheep, have gone astray; each of us has turned to his own way; AND THE LORD HAS LAID ON HIM the iniquity of us all." *Isaiah 53:6*

"HE IS THE ATONING SACRIFICE for our sins: and not only for ours but also for the sins of the whole world." *1 John 2:2*

"For Christ died for sins ONCE FOR ALL, the RIGHTEOUS for the UNRIGHTEOUS, to bring you to God." *1 Peter 3:18*

"You see, at just the right time, when we were still powerless, Christ died for the UNGODLY...But God demonstrates his own love for us in this: while we were still sinners, CHRIST DIED FOR US." *Romans 5:6 & 8.*

"For the Son of Man came to SEEK and to SAVE what was lost." *Luke 19:10*

"IT IS FINISHED." *John 19:30*

FREE TRACT SOCIETY
P.O. Box 50531 · Los Angeles, CA 90050

# KEEP THESE THOUGHTS BEFORE YOU
# AND REMEMBER

1. **That you may be saved** - "For God so loved the world that he gave his one and only Son, that whoever believes in him shall not perish but have eternal life." - John 3:16.

2. **That Salvation is free.**-"Come, all you who are thirsty, come to the waters; and you who have no money, come, buy and eat! Come, buy wine and milk without money and without cost." - Isaiah 55:1

3. **That God does not license sin.**-"The soul who sins is the one who will die." - Ezekiel 18:4. "He who does what is sinful is of the devil" - 1 John 3:8

4. **That God is just, and sin must be punished.** - "For the wages of sin is death."- Romans 6:23. "Then death and Hades were thrown into the lake of fire. The lake of fire is the second death. If anyone's name was not found written in the book of life, he was thrown into the lake of fire." Revelation 20:14-15. "The wicked return to the grave, all the nations that forget God." - Psalm 9:17

5. **That God sees your very acts** [whether in thought, word or deed]-you cannot hide them from him, "There is nothing concealed that will not be disclosed, or hidden that will not be made known." - Matthew 10:26

6. **That every Blessing you enjoy in the life, even the air you breathe, comes from God.** Have you thanked Him for them? "Let everything that has breath praise the Lord. Praise the Lord." - Psalm 150:6

7. **That you have been placed here on earth to serve God;** and not the devil.-"Worship the Lord your God, and serve him only." - Matthew 4:10

8. **That your future life depends upon what you make of the present.** "Do not be deceived: God cannot be mocked. A man reaps what he sows." - Galatians 6:7

# ACCEPT CHRIST NOW!

creature, given to quaint chants and cadences of voice, with a delivery alternating between breathless patter and the measured, tolling strokes of a bell. Her languorous postures, her gestures, feverish or stately, her whole *plastik*, are parts of an elaborate harmony. What she aims at is beauty. Now Signora Duse's aim is truth, the whole truth and nothing but the truth. She is absolutely natural and sincere. Her gestures are not in stage arabesques and 'lines of beauty', but in the abrupt re-entrant angles of actual life.[19]

Duse, like Réjane, introduced a different performance style, and critics rushed to either defend Sarah's histrionic method or to welcome the break with tradition with marked enthusiasm. As Duse breathed new life into familiar heroines – Marguerite, Fedora, Cleopatra – her simple, intellectual and human approach excited those, such as Shaw, who decried the 'artificial' and 'exotic'. Although Duse did not possess Réjane's irregular features, she was a plain and frail woman who did not seek to colour her person with cosmetics, costumes or elaborate settings. Hence, she was far less suited to certain roles (Cleopatra, for example) than Sarah with her exotic trappings and beauty.

The tension and rivalry mounted as the two actresses took to creating the same new roles. In 1894 Bernhardt created Césarine in Dumas's *La Femme de Claude* which Duse offered the following year in her London season of plays. An examination of both interpretations highlights where the new intellectual spirit conflicted with the need for the exotic and the passionate, rather than the natural and the simple.

*La Femme de Claude* was written in conjunction with Dumas's misogynistic pamphlet in support of the 'Tue-la' doctrine, in which it is stated that a husband has the right to kill an evil, wayward wife. The 'moral blood thirstiness' of the dramatic theme was greeted unsympathetically by English critics and audiences. There was far too much debate, and the dramatic action, where it existed, was melodramatic in the extreme. In brief, Césarine, a woman of loose morals, attempts to steal her husband's plans for the invention of a new firearm by seducing and coercing his pupil into criminal collaboration, for which the husband shoots her and walks away with his pupil to carry on with his work. As 'the beast of the Apocalypse', 'a species of human vermin', Césarine the anti-heroine was not a part in

107

which Bernhardt's admirers welcomed her.[20] It was never to become a popular or regular role in her repertoire.[21] Despite the antipathetic nature of Césarine, Bernhardt found a means of superimposing her own note of pathos on the author's conception, thereby rendering the heroine more sympathetic:

> It is difficult to understand the real nature of the erring wife, who, after having sinned and been forgiven, and afterwards sinned again and again, comes and professes the most profound penitence and begs to be taken back to her husband's affections. Such is the influence of Madame Sarah Bernhardt's truthful style of acting, that one is led to infer that the penitence is real; yet it is by no means clear that such is the intention of the author.[22]

As Sarah characterised Césarine with a tiger-like ferocity and seductive temperament, the focal point became the display of her range of emotion rather than any real sense of the 'Tue-la' doctrine.

Duse's style and physique were far less compatible with this type of 'modern Messalina' than Bernhardt's. She had neither the seductive nor the passionate temperament of Sarah, and simplicity and naturalness were not enough to suggest the incarnation of a *bête noire*. It was argued that 'Cesarina is just as likely to have been the plain, brown little rebel represented by Duse, as a kind of modern Cleopatra', though this concession was tempered with a warning about her method being too 'small' in its 'ultra-naturalness' for the 'romantic breadth' of the piece.[23] Critics were surprised to find that she was able to represent the 'Delilah allurement' to a greater degree than had been anticipated,[24] though again, this inadvertently points towards the underlying implication of a fundamental incompatibility between her method, looks and role.

Clearly, therefore, where a ferocious and passionate temperament were prerequisites of an interpretation, Duse tended to put herself at a disadvantage. The London productions of *Magda* in 1895, which the two actresses played within two days of each other – Sarah on 10 June and Duse on 12 June – placed them on a more equal footing and enabled critics to isolate the merits of each. *Magda*, in both the French and Italian versions, is a translation of the German play *Heimat* by Sudermann. The original focuses on the overbearing father-figure Schwartz, and as the action begins, it is made known that he ousted his daughter Magda from the family home when she refused to co-operate in an arranged marriage. The play shows Magda returning to the homestead now that she has made her name and fortune as a singer. The contrast between Magda's current good fortune and the poverty of the home she left is established in the early scenes. The past catches up with the heroine as she encounters an erstwhile lover (now a Councillor of State) who had left her when she became pregnant. On learning of his daughter's past, Schwartz insists that Magda marry her former lover, but she refuses. The angry father attempts to carry out Dumas's 'Tue-la' doctrine on his daughter, but in attempting to do so, he has a stroke, leaving Magda alive and ready to carry on with her career.

The change in title from *Heimat* to *Magda* indicates a significant change in dramatic emphasis which both actresses reinforced in their performances. The antipathetic father-figure which dominates the German play was mercifully played down in both the Italian and French versions. Spurred on by a sense of rivalry, Sarah was on brilliant form in *Magda*. Her heroine had the look of a woman who might have just spent twelve years in the theatre and was invested with a Bohemian spirit of life, love and suffering. By contrast, Duse's Magda lacked the carefree spirit of the artistic world, and was characterised instead by a virtuous veneer. When she met with her ex-lover, it was as though she had never ceased to love him, and her awkwardness and delicacy of feeling were signified by a natural feat of blushing which Shaw recollected in glowing terms.[25] Sarah, on the other hand, made it plain that she had dismissed the man from her heart and had had many lovers in the intervening years.

Reviewers were divided over who achieved the more apt cry of maternal anguish when the mother in Magda is insulted by the ex-lover's proposal to marry her but to disown the child. A very few more critics preferred Sarah's maternal anguish, while they also recognised that this was an unusual note to find among her customarily childless heroines. Each of the Magdas established a motive for returning home, Sarah's out of curiosity and Duse's out of concern for her younger sister, still subject to the adverse effects of patriarchal authority.

Overall, the majority of critics were delighted at the opportunity of seeing the two styles side by side and appreciated the differences and the best qualities of each, without stooping to pit one against the other. Those who did favour the French style suggested that Duse was ill-placed in the Bernhardtesque roles and was struggling to triumph against the grain. On the other hand, those who supported the anti-Bernhardt stance – spearheaded by Bernard Shaw – argued that Duse's plainness simply showed that her dramatic genius did not depend on looks but on talent.[26]

It was attitudes such as this that fuelled the comparative debate which was hotly pursued into the twentieth century. Duse began the new century with a programme of plays by her lover Gabriele D'Annunzio, which included the costly failure *Francesca da Rimini*, premièred in Rome in December 1901, but which she nevertheless succeeded in establishing in her repertoire and brought to London's Adelphi in 1903. Sarah followed her example with Marion Crawford's *Francesca da Rimini* (translated by Marcel Schwob and Eugène Morand) which opened at her own theatre in April 1902 and was brought to London two months later. Both had plenty of faults to overcome: Duse had to deal with D'Annunzio's excessively long and violent composition; Sarah, with all her charms, struggled to redress the play's explicit sympathy for the husband Giovanni Malatesta in favour of Francesca and her lover Paolo and to steal some of the limelight back from M. de Max, who received glowing reviews for his performance as the husband.

This cross-section of European actresses shows both the imitators of Sarah's histrionic method and the challenge of the new styles from younger rivals. Among those who followed Sarah's tradition and method, like Modjeska or Mrs Bernard-Beere, none reached the heights of her dramatic genius. As advocates of the new increased in numbers during the last decade of the old century, Sarah maintained her star-status by virtue of her consummate histrionic talent which enabled her to survive even the fiercest hostility from critics like Shaw. One would not wish to deny the genius of either Réjane or Duse but simply to argue their difference. Critical prejudices in some ways did more harm than good by forcing the issue of rivalry, particularly in the case of

Bernhardt and Duse, where international star status and contrasting styles and images fuelled a constant note of competition between the two actresses. This perhaps explains why Sarah and Ellen Terry shared a mutual respect for one another's very different repertoires and why, when Sarah has a good word for Bartet, Réjane and Mrs Pat in her *Mémoires*, she is highly critical of Duse.[27]

The wide range of actresses visiting London also shows how cosmopolitan and international the capital's stage had become. This was brought home in 1900 when the London stage received a season of drama from a Japanese company who went on to the Paris exhibition and returned to London for a further season in 1901. A report in the *Star* heralded the leading actress of the troupe, Sada Yocco, as the 'Bernhardt of Japan' and proceeded to explain the emotionalist style of the Japanese actress in Bernhardtesque terms.[28] How interesting, that when the dramatic East met the West it should have been in a style which, with its lovers' duels, jealous rivals and martyred heroines, was immediately recognisable and decodable as a histrionic method à la Bernhardt.

# Notes

1. See Arthur Symonds, *Eleonora Duse* (New York & London: Benjamin Blom, 1969), pp. 73–4.
2. *Era*, 18 June 1881.
3. *Daily Telegraph*, 7 May 1883.
4. *The Times*, 10 July 1889.
5. *Daily Telegraph*, 27 May 1895.
6. *The Theatrical World of 1895* (London: Walter Scott, 1896), p. 174.
7. Edith Craig and Christopher St John, eds, *Ellen Terry's Memoirs* (London: Victor Gollancz, 1933), p. 168.
8. Ibid., p. 125.
9. J.T. Grein, *Dramatic Criticism 1902–3* (London: Eveleigh Nash, 1904), p. 260.
10. Ibid.
11. *Westminster Gazette*, 30 June 1903.
12. *Pall Mall Gazette*, 31 July 1888.

13. Max Beerbohm, *Last Theatres 1904–10* (London: Rupert Hart Davis, 1970), pp. 370–3.
14. Ibid., p. 372.
15. Ibid.
16. Robert H. Sherard, 'Madame Réjane', *Lady's Realm* (July 1899), pp. 293–301.
17. For details of Réjane's signification of *le peuple*, see John Stokes, 'A Kind of Beauty: Réjane in London', *Themes in Drama*, 6, ed. James Redmond (Cambridge: Cambridge University Press, 1984), pp. 97–119.
18. Kate Terry Gielgud, *A Victorian Playgoer* (London: Heinemann, 1980), p. 60.
19. *Speaker*, 27 May 1893.
20. *Star*, 18 July 1894.
21. During her London seasons, it was revived in 1898 when Sarah performed it on a double bill with Octave Feuillet's *Julie*. This was a heavy programme, with the 'tue-la' doctrine followed by the depressing tableau of *Julie*, in which a distressed mother and neglected wife dies decrying her husband and defending her lover whom she believes to be dead. Audiences and critics found the programme too long and too depressing, and the double bill lasted for only two nights (30 and 31 May).
22. *Daily News*, 18 July 1894.
23. *Era*, 8 June 1895.
24. *Westminster Gazette*, 6 June 1895.
25. See Shaw's essay, 'Duse and Bernhardt' in *Shaw's Dramatic Criticism (1895–98)*, ed. John F. Matthews (Westport, CT: Greenwood Press, 1959), pp. 80–6.
26. Central to Shaw's attacks on Sarah were his frequent references to her over-use of make-up. That Sarah was to a certain degree susceptible to his criticism and aware of the praise for Duse's unadorned features is indicated in Shaw's review of her Mélissinde in *La Princesse lointaine* which followed *Magda*, where he claims the make-up 'had all but disappeared' (*Shaw's Dramatic Criticism*, pp. 86–94). Similarly, in an article for *Cosmopolitan*, March 1896, 530–2, Sarah claimed to rely less on make-up and more on 'facial expression', an exaggerated claim but indicative of her sensitiveness to the criticisms.
27. Sarah Bernhardt, *Mémoires*, vol. II, pp. 134–5.
28. *Star*, 5 June 1901.

# 7 Male Guises

As a mature actress, Sarah's quest for new material proved increasingly difficult. Given her star status, she could rely on her repertoire of earlier years, as these were the roles which, despite her advancing years, audiences still clamoured for. Spectators consistently and constantly demanded her victim-heroines and rebuffed her various attempts at the more matronly or maternal types. Although she was not as slight as she had been in her youth, she retained an agile and graceful figure and had a face which belied the advancement of her years. Ultimately, Sarah resolved the problem of finding new parts by making use of these natural gifts in *travesti* roles. So at an age and time when many actresses either gracefully accepted defeat by taking a back seat in minor roles or got married and left the stage altogether, Sarah was able to increase her range of roles and deploy her talents in new ventures.

The tradition of the *travesti* role on the French stage was alien to the English. The tradition of the 'breeches role' in opera burlesque, music-halls and in the principal boys of Victorian and Edwardian pantomime was accepted, popular and flourishing, but on the 'legitimate' stage, it was considered very daring and risqué for an actress to appear in male attire. Actresses appearing in Shakespearean roles such as Rosalind or Viola, where the plot demanded the woman disguise herself as a youth, had to take care with their dress and deportment in order not to offend audience sensibilities. This prudish prejudice was hard to break. As late as 1920, Mrs Patrick Campbell records the offence caused when she wore trousers for her interpretation of Mme Sand in a play based on the writer's life.

By contrast, the tradition of *travesti* in France had become an established dramatic convention from the eighteenth century onwards and did not shock or cause offence. As May Agate writes in her reflections on Sarah Bernhardt and the French theatre: 'Now it has always seemed somewhat incongruous to the English mind that women should play male rôles, but no such prejudice

113

exists in France. From Beaumarchais's Chérubin onwards, adolescent manhood has been represented on the French stage by women players, and it must be understood that *le travesti*, as they call it, has not been merely permissible but customary.'[1] The tradition was revitalised when the French actress, Virginie Déjazet, launched a successful vaudeville career at the Palais Royal in the 1830s. During her lifetime she impersonated great French men such as Rousseau, Voltaire and Napoleon and finally, at the age of 62, played the male lead in Sardou's *Monsieur Garat*.

Just as Déjazet's career was coming to a close, Sarah Bernhardt was tasting her first success in the highly acclaimed *travesti* role Zanetto in Coppée's *Le Passant* (1869). It was perhaps the triumph of this success which provided her with the idea of creating more adolescent heros later on in her career. Unfortunately, the wandering minstrel clad in an Arthurian floral jerkin and tights – head crowned with a blond wavy wig and feathered hat – was not a male guise which Sarah established in her London repertoire, despite its Parisian success. Although the role is characterised by asexuality and an androgynous, child-like innocence, Sarah was perhaps too conscious of English prejudices and tastes to risk causing offence when she first sought to conquer her London audiences. It was therefore restricted to private salon performances, and in June 1881 she performed it on a benefit evening for Madame Modjeska. The one *travesti* performance which she offered as part of her repertoire in these early years was the young Edouard in *Les enfants d'Edouard*. This was acceptable to English audiences because the roles of the princes were numbered among the juvenile parts undertaken by child-actresses. As a young girl, Ellen Terry, for instance, proved a very successful Duke of York.[2] Furthermore, as the historical drama focuses on matters of state, it avoids the love or courtship interest (central to the role of Zanetto) and could not possibly be construed as offensive or indelicate. However, the interest shown in Sarah's young Edouard was lukewarm, when compared to her petticoated heroines Adrienne and Gilberte, whose contemporary appearance suggested that the magnetism of Sarah's 'sex appeal' in her major female roles was far greater than that of her androgynous image.

The convention of playing adolescent heros which Sarah essayed in her formative years – including *Les Premières armes de Richelieu* (Richelieu), *Athalie* (Zacharie), *Le Mariage de Figaro* (Chérubin) and *Pierrot assassin* (Pierrot) – was developed in subsequent years when Sarah embarked on more complex male roles, above and beyond the limitations of traditional *travesti*. To her London and Paris audiences she offered three major male impersonations: *Lorenzaccio*, *Hamlet* and *L'Aiglon*. Bernhardt referred to them as the three Hamlets: 'the black Hamlet of Shakespeare, the white Hamlet of Rostand's *L'Aiglon* and the Florentine Hamlet of Alfred de Musset's *Lorenzaccio*'.[3] She justified her undertaking of these male parts in two ways. Firstly she outlined the kind of male roles suitable for women to play, stating that 'a woman cannot interpret a male role, unless it consists of a strong mind in a weak body'.[4] As examples of male roles women cannot play she cites Napoleon, Don Juan and Romeo. What lies behind this notion is the idea that women are suited to androgynous asexual roles, but not to those which require manliness and virility. Romeo is perhaps an odd choice, for the sexual coupling in *Romeo and Juliet* is secondary to the signification of spiritual 'Romance' at its most tragic height. Certainly at one stage Sarah had contemplated a production of *Romeo and Juliet* with Maude Adams as Juliet, but this did not come to fruition, which might account for Sarah's self-defensive inclusion of the role in her anti-*travesti* list.

Secondly, Sarah explains why women are actually better suited than men to the roles she outlines as appropriate for *travesti*, an argument set out in an article for the American magazine *Harper's Bazaar*:

> There is one important reason why I think a woman is better adapted to play parts like *L'Aiglon* and *Hamlet* than a man. These rôles portray youths of twenty or twenty-one, with the minds of men of forty. A boy of twenty cannot understand the philosophy of *Hamlet*, nor the poetic enthusiasm of *L'Aiglon*, and without understanding there is no delineation of character. There are no young men of that age capable of playing these parts, consequently an older man essays the rôle. He does not look the boy, nor has he the ready adaptability of the woman, who can combine the light carriage of youth with the mature thought of the man. The woman more readily looks the part and yet has the maturity of mind to grasp it.[5]

115

What Bernhardt describes is a kind of thinking Peter Pan: maturity of thought combined with physical asexuality, which is a characteristic of her Hamlet types.

Bernhardt put her theory of an old head on young shoulders into practice with the first of her more complex *travesti* roles in *Lorenzaccio* at the Renaissance in 1896. The adaptation turned Musset's study in tyranny, into 'Boulevard melodrama' and transformed the prince, ultimately defeated by the corrupt Medici power he set out to destroy, into the sensationalised role of 'avenging liberator'.[6] The role of 'avenging liberator', whatever its sensationalist appeal to audiences, did not hoodwink the critics, who did not agree with her conception of Lorenzaccio and the betrayal of Musset's original intention, though they conceded that the merit of the production lay solely in her performance, and some paid high tribute to her art of *travesti*.

Sarah brought *Lorenzaccio* to London in the 1897 season. The lengthy and fragmentary drama – held together by the somewhat melodramatic, Brutus–Hamlet figure – was even harder for English audiences to follow than for the French. Although the play was universally disliked, Sarah's *travesti* performance generated a great deal of critical interest, and the role, for all its shortcomings, afforded the opportunity for a variety of moods and emotions suited to Sarah's performance skills:

> Nothing could be better than the sad, enigmatic, languishing, and disdainful air which she assumes, or than her brief shudders under her mask of cowardice, her insolent and diabolical irony, her absorption in a fixed idea, the hysteria of her vengeance, and the artificial means of excitement by which she nerves herself to act. And then we have her pauses of tenderness and her periods of dreaming, her appalling despair, and lastly, the supreme somnambulistic rehearsal of the approaching scene of the murder.[7]

On her first appearance Sarah was costumed in 'sables of the deepest dye'. Her doublet and hose were black to suit the sombre tone of the piece, though Kate Terry Gielgud for one thought her attire unbecoming and objected both to her 'full figure and slight limbs' in 'masculine garb' and, with the exception of her fencing scene, to the ungainly use of her arms.[8] Another suggested that Sarah's 'stouter' figure was the reason for the omission of textual references to the prince's 'excessive leanness'.[9] Overall, the critics were divided over how successful they considered the illusion of maleness. In the more flattering reviews, it was conceded that the illusion worked and that Sarah could captivate an audience without having to emphasise her female charm. The opposite view proposed that Sarah's 'greatness lies in her sex, and that when she dons the breeches she loses her individuality'.[10] That Sarah was striving for 'maleness' and the suppression of femininity was further evidenced in her voice, as the golden tones (sorely missed by some) were replaced by a 'strange guttural' effect in order to masculinise her vocal delivery.

Undaunted by her 'Florentine Hamlet', Bernhardt launched her Shakespearean Hamlet on the Parisian public, who sat through the five-hour production in May 1899. The following month she presented it to the London public, who were curious and concerned to see what she would do to their Danish prince. The Parisian press had not been over-enthusiastic about the May production at Sarah's theatre but had shown clemency by commenting on edited highlights which they felt to be successful. The London critics shared their lack of enthusiasm, and as the translation (faithfully executed by Eugène Morand and Marcel Schwob) was still overlong, the first night audience was rather restless, and not for the first time was 'We won't go home 'til morning' whistled from the gallery.

The hostility of the English press was inspired both by Bernhardt's unconventional interpretation of the part and by the idea of a woman (and a French woman at that) playing Shakespeare's melancholy prince. She was not the first French actress to do so; Mme Judith had played the part in 1867. Although there had been a few English female Hamlets since Mrs Siddons, who had the dubious honour of being the first in a line which included Mrs Inchbald (1780), Mrs Powell (1796), Julia Glover (1821) and Alice Marriott (1861), these interpretations were recalled as risqué novelties rather than viewed as a serious *travesti* tradition. Later, in the 1890s, Mrs Bandmann-Palmer played the part frequently in the provinces, and in 1899 Bernhardt was rivalling the Hamlet of Clara Howard (Mrs George Daventry), who heightened the sense of novelty by playing Hamlet as melodrama in the Mile End Road.

117

The *Daily Telegraph* opened its review with comparative comments on one of the earlier English female Hamlets and Bernhardt's current attempt. Miss Alice Mariott's Hamlet, the reviewer noted, had been remarkable for the voice but not for the figure. Her ample proportions 'opposed the popular idea of what the Prince should be', and her performance was remarkable wholly for its 'flattering exhibition of pure elocutionary methods'.[12] In contrast, Sarah's relatively slighter figure suited the part, as 'it is the wispy, willowy Hamlet who best conforms to our predilections'. The review echoed Bernhardt's theory of youthful looks and maturity of interpretation, noting that in general Hamlets had either one or the other and that it was rare to find a combination of the two.

As Sarah explained in the *Harper's Bazaar* article, she was adamant that a successful male impersonation depended upon the audience believing the actress to 'actually be the boy' and not to sit in judgement on how well she played the part. To this end, she placed great emphasis on the actress's build and the importance of not being overweight. Although the *Daily Telegraph* was impressed by the suitability of her physical proportions, others were less satisfied. The *Era*, both thoroughly disappointed and outraged by her attempt, saw too much of Bernhardt's own sex in her Hamlet, writing: 'As a Male Impersonator, Mme Bernhardt is a dire failure. Indeed, to say otherwise would be to cruelly fault her. For it is only the unsexed woman, the woman, who, physically and physiologically, approaches to the masculine – the monstrosity in short – that can deceive us as to her gender on the stage.'[13] Because, the reviewer continued, Sarah was 'distinctly feminine', her attempted masculinity, such as cocking her legs up on a couch, her 'manly stride' or 'gruff growlings', resulted in the portrait of an 'angry elderly woman' and not a 'young and emotional man'. It failed because the illusion had been absent from the beginning, and the reviewer was finally driven to quoting Johnson's homily on the dancing dog (that could not dance well, though it was a wonder it could dance at all). The review reveals the widespread prejudicial attitude towards the idea of women playing men's roles and a highly conservative view of the image of women. If a woman is not beautiful and feminine, then she is considered an aberration of her sex.

118

As the reviewer states that boy parts (of the kind traditionally found in pantomime or those suitable for child-actresses) may be played by women because the sexes are not so distinct in youth, it is clear that Hamlet was not bracketed in this category. The French public had simply decoded Bernhardt's later Hamlet types as more complex versions of her earlier conventional *travesti* parts based on a youthful and asexual image, but for the English critics, Hamlet was a more 'manly' type, which is why the role had generally been conceived as unsuitable for serious, female interpretation, unless the actress was 'phenomenally masculine' and hence a freak. This attitude coloured many critical opinions. The American actress Elizabeth Robins, assessing her fellow actress's performance, states that she 'had no idea that I was about to be convinced that women cannot "do" men's parts', and her assessment of Bernhardt's endeavours reveals that, in her opinion, Bernhardt fell very short of actually 'being' the boy:

> However well she does it (and I do not believe it could be better done than in the instance under consideration), there is no moment in the drama when the spectator is not fully and calmly conscious that the hero is a woman masquerading, or is jarred into sharp realization of the fact by her doing something that is very like a man . . . Madame Bernhardt's assumption of masculinity is so cleverly carried out that one loses sight of Hamlet in one's admiration of the *tour de force* of the actress. This is not to say that she gives us a man, but rather Sarah Bernhardt playing with amazing skill, a spirited boy; doing it with an impetuosity, a youthfulness, almost childish.[14]

She cites the scenes with Ophelia as being particularly problematic in the context of male impersonation, thereby underlining a discrepancy between Bernhardt's notion of a strong mind and feeble body and her own more virile reading of the Danish prince.

Max Beerbohm, who opened his review with, 'I cannot, on my heart, take Sarah's Hamlet seriously', expands on this view.[15] He assumes that Sarah's reason for essaying the part rests on her understanding of Hamlet's 'gentleness' and his 'lack of executive ability' as distinctly 'feminine qualities', but her reasoning thereby failed to recognise that 'Hamlet is none the less a man because he is not consistently manly, just as Lady Macbeth is none the less a woman for being a trifle unsexed . . . Sarah ought not to have supposed that Hamlet's weakness set him in any

119

possible relation to her own feminine mind and body'.[16] Sarah, on the other hand, conceived Hamlet as an 'unsexed being', who 'must be stripped of all virility' in order to reveal the anguish of the soul which 'burns the body'.[17] In other words, a healthy, masculine and virile torso was not, according to Sarah, an appropriate external signifier of Hamlet's inner torment.

American critic John Hansen felt it unlikely that English audiences could possibly comprehend the French Hamlet, as different to Shakespeare's as Paris was different to London. More generous in his praise than several of the English critics, Hansen found her physique sufficiently sexless for the role but facially too feminine:

> Physically Bernhardt's unusual lines of figure proved of assistance in rendering her impersonation sexless if not altogether masculine. Even now, with a contour rounded out considerably since the days when the supreme dramatic genius of our times was better known to the American public, Bernhardt, costumed in the traditional sables of the Dane, does not belie the part by a strong suggestion of femininity except facially; there she comes up against a stumbling block – that elderly, unique face, haunting at any time, becomes a nightmare, a spectre in opposition to her faithful simulation of a youth's body.[18]

His description of her ever youthful but fuller figure compared to earlier years is more accurate than adjectives such as 'willowy', and is substantiated by photographic evidence (see Illustration 6). As in the case of her Lorenzaccio, Kate Terry Gielgud considered her 'stolid' appearance as unbecoming, and Beerbohm would have preferred her 'sable doublet and hose' to have been confiscated by the customs officials at Charing Cross. Clearly, the English prejudice with regard to male impersonation was hard to break.

Sarah's voice also came under close scrutiny and attack. As in her impersonation of the Florentine prince, she introduced a note of harshness as an attempted stab at masculinity, though the majority of reviewers would have much rather she stuck to her golden tones, whatever the distraction from the illusion of maleness. Suze Rueff, Sarah's Dutch companion, claims that the harsh registers were in fact the result of her dogged enemy, stage-fright, from which, she claims, there was no doubt Bernhardt suffered on her opening night in London. While stage-fright 'somewhat marred the beauty of her voice', Rueff claimed, it brought into play, 'that perfect technique, the result of long years of assiduous training, which enabled her to master forth a semblance of self-assurance that in reality she was far from experiencing'.[19] Rueff notes that one critic at least commented on her 'self possession' (this was in fact Beerbohm), and one of the more positive points that Elizabeth Robins made about her performance was the presence of gestural control:

> her wonderful mastery of sheer *poise*; that power she has of standing stock still for an indefinite length of time with perfect ease and grace, never shifting her ground, and equally never ceasing for a moment to be dramatic. It was when she stood so, her feet firmly planted, making only occasional use of sparing, clean-cut gesture, that she came nearest, I should say, to the effect that the artist in her wanted to produce.[20]

As was the case on the occasion of her Lady Macbeth, Sarah might have received more favourable reviews, if her English critics had been able to conquer their own prejudicial conception of the melancholic prince. Because she chose to depict the prince as a young man who conceals his heartache by the smile on his lips, she was found wanting in 'proper philosophical melancholy'. This was the crux of English criticism, which expressed the view that the impetuous spirited youth was a travesty of the pensive prince, and the purists reminded her that this was Shakespeare – not Sardou. An enlightened few found her conception of the character refreshing, like Clement Scott or *The Times*, which welcomed her 'vigour and interest' and her 'pleasant, humorous, very gay prince, who in happier circumstances would have been the life and soul of the Court'.[21]

If the overall conception offended, there were at least moments of stage business which were generally recognised as original and imaginative, notably the 'buzz buzz' scenes with Polonius which Bernhardt turned into a make-believe game of fly-catching, the play scene and that of her thrusting a torch into the face of the guilty uncle, or the tableau of Hamlet demonstrating filial affection by kissing the streaming hair of his dying mother. Stimulating moments of original stagecraft, perhaps, but not enough to convince the English critics of the merits of her male impersonation.

Neither Bernhardt's Hamlet nor her Lorenzaccio were great box-office draws, either in England or France. Not so her *travesti* role in Rostand's *L'Aiglon*, her 'white Hamlet', which opened the following year, 15 March 1900, at the Théâtre Sarah Bernhardt. Rostand's six-act, verse play, based on the short life of Napoleon's son, is excruciating to read and hard to imagine as a box-office winner. Nevertheless, the play was a huge success due to Rostand's choice of interpreter (he had in fact written the play with Bernhardt in mind) and the play's intense evocation of nationalism. Coming, as it did, after the divisions of the Dreyfus affair and coinciding with the *Exposition Universelle*, it was a significant theatrical event in terms of the patriotism which it inspired.

Napoleonic fervour set to alexandrine verse was less likely to appeal to an English audience, and spectators experienced a certain amount of difficulty in following the history and language of the French nation. Its reception, however, benefitted from the number of French spectators in the audience – reciprocating the number of curious English spectators who had attended the Hamlet première in Paris.

Bernhardt drew her own parallels between Hamlet and the duc de Reichstadt as sons 'bewildered by unworthy mothers'.[22] L' Aiglon, like Hamlet, is stuck in a world in which he cannot act because he is subject to the constraints of the Austrian court and is haunted, not by an assassinated father, but by one whom the world would have him believe did not exist. Where the boyish tones and youthful insolence had failed in *Hamlet*, they succeeded in *L'Aiglon*, and she sustained the illusion of the part from the early scenes as the Eaglet plays with his army of toy soldiers, painted in the outlawed colours of Napoleon's guards, to the final death scene, acted with tremendous pathos in the presence of the frivolous mother.

Whereas the English critics had strongly objected to the idea of a non-virile Hamlet, her conception of a weak body and tortured mind applied more readily to the consumptive L'Aiglon, whose feverish contemplations on his own inadequacies result in premature death. They recognised the womanish nature of his character, a youth who is 'three-parts a woman, with spasms of delirium and a power of rapid and passionate rhetoric',[23] as more in keeping with Sarah's physique, skills and sex. Though she again injected a harsher note into her voice, a boyish lyricism was in greater evidence and was more pleasing to the ear. Arthur Symonds wrote of the musicality of her voice, her 'liquid articulation of every syllable', describing her as an actress who 'never forgets that art is not nature, and that when one is speaking verse one is not talking prose'.[24] As in Rostand's *La Princesse lointaine*, Sarah spoke the verse with a far greater beauty than was to be found in the poet's words themselves, and the effect, despite the language barrier, was not lost on her audience.

Whereas the French critics had allowed themselves to be carried away by the spell-binding magic of their great French actress conjuring up the Napoleonic ghost, the English still sat in judgement upon a woman playing a man's role. Yet at another level they were full of admiration for her accomplishment in the exacting part and were impressed by the energy and variety of her performance. The huge cast of *L'Aiglon* is entirely peripheral to the characters of L'Aiglon and the old Napoleonic campaigner, Flambeau. Sarah was fortunate enough to have secured the talents of Coquelin to support her in this other key role – the appearance of the great French actor playing alongside her added further publicity and appeal to the London production. Coquelin's accomplishment in the part was highly commended, though inevitably overshadowed by detailed analysis of Sarah's performance. Having engaged Coquelin to perform in *L'Aiglon* throughout the whole of June, Sarah relinquished some of the limelight by agreeing to four July performances of Rostand's best-remembered play, *Cyrano de Bergerac*, playing the lesser, petticoated role of Roxane to Coquelin's Cyrano, and at the end of the season organised a double bill of *Phèdre*, for herself, and *Les Prècieuses ridicules*, for Coquelin.

It was rumoured the following year that Sarah had plans to appear as Lancelot in a translation of Comyn Carr's *Arthur*, but this project did not materialise. At her theatre in Paris in March 1903, she played the male lead in a stage version of Goethe's *Werther*, adapted by Pierre Decourcelle, with incidental music by Reynaldo Hahn. It was a dull piece, marred by the difficulties of adaptation, and although Sarah's Werther, akin to her sorrowing, mournful L'Aiglon, was a creditable impersonation, she was not tempted to bring the play to London. Instead, she offered her English audiences a much lighter role from the *travesti* genre in the one-act play *Bohèmos*. The twenty-year-old, penniless poet Bohèmos is a conventional *travesti* role. Sarah produced the play on tour in Monte Carlo in the spring of 1903 and then brought it to London in June. It was performed after an exacting matinée of *Andromaque*, in which Sarah finally played the more demanding role of Hermione, and provided a delightful, light-hearted contrast to the sombre world of the Racinian tragedy. The one-act *fantaisie* by Miguel Zumacois depicts the poverty-stricken Bohèmos in love with Leonida, who takes a rich husband whom the two lovers then proceed to dupe out of his money. The role gave Sarah the opportunity to display a pleasing figure as the 'romantic youth' and to show, somewhat unusually, the actress in the light and mischievous mood of comedy. As the plot avoided a sexual union between Leonida and Bohèmos, it did not threaten to cause offence. Despite the *Daily Telegraph* reviewer's appreciation of Sarah's 'comic genius' and assertion that the 'little play should assuredly be accorded a prominent place in her repertoire',[25] the play was not kept on – presumably it was of too slight a nature to be other than a *divertissement* for Sarah.

Sarah pursued her interest in romantic Arthurian *travesti* the following year when she played the prince in Maeterlinck's *Pelléas et Mélisande* in July 1904. The production attracted a lot of attention because it brought together the talents of Bernhardt and Mrs Patrick Campbell, who played Mélisande. Mrs Campbell had already demonstrated her beauty and talent in the part, in the 1898 production at the Prince of Wales Theatre with Forbes Robertson and Martin Harvey. Bernhardt had taken a box at the first matinée and had been able to see Mrs Campbell's Mélisande for herself. However, playing opposite Bernhardt's Pelléas entailed the added difficulty for Mrs Patrick Campbell of speaking the part in French. Though familiar with the language and the French text, she had some difficulty with her pronunciation, but Bernhardt felt that this simply served to enhance the 'dream-like' quality of Maeterlinck's play.

Because of the play's fantasy setting and treatment of the

eternal triangle theme, transposed to a landscape of the imagination, the role of Pelléas was appropriate for male impersonation. Pelléas is the mythological white knight, the desirable 'prince of love' destined to fail in the quest for his love-object, which is tragically kept from him by greater and unseen forces. There are few indications of physical passion which would detract from the image of asexual and adolescent charm; love simply hangs in unfinished sentences and pregnant pauses.

For the production Mrs Campbell wore the shimmering gold dress (nicknamed the 'gold umbrella case') designed by Burne-Jones, which she wore in the original 1898 performance, and with her long tresses of hair the overall effect was that of the fairy-tale princess. She made particular use of the long hair in the window scene of the third act, in which Mélisande shakes her locks so that they tumble over Pelléas's face, a piece of stage-business successfully carried out by the two actresses and one which heightened the fairy-tale connotations, by its affinity with the Rapunzel tale of the princess trapped in the tower, who lets down her hair for her lover riding by in the forest.

Sarah, on the other hand, strove to create a suitable princely exterior. She wore a surcoat of chain-mail designed by Graham Robertson. With her tunic, tights and page-boy curls, she had the look of a young Raphael. That this adolescent youth was now in reality a woman of sixty and his princess a comparably aging actress attracted some criticism and caused another admirer, Max Beerbohm, to stay away:

> I love the play too well, and am loth that my memory of it as performed by Mrs Campbell in her own language, with Mr Martin Harvey as Pelléas, should be complicated with any memory less pleasing. I am quite willing to assume that Mrs Campbell speaks French as exquisitely as she speaks English, and that Sarah's Pelléas is not, like her Hamlet and her Duc de Reichstadt, merely ladylike. But the two facts remain that Sarah is a woman and that Mrs Campbell is an Englishwoman. And by these two facts, such a performance is ruled out of the sphere of art into the sphere of sensationalism. If Maeterlinck were a sensationalist, that would not matter.[26]

The attack on the concept of male impersonation was still very strong. The *Pall Mall Gazette* reviewer, who expanded at length on the displeasing vision of a Pelléas who was a good deal shorter than Mélisande, went on to expound on the degeneration of Sarah's Pelléas into a mere 'Principal Boy'.[27] Because, in his opinion, the character was 'effeminate', it needed to be masculinised by a male presence. On the other hand, there were those who considered that Pelléas, played by a woman, supported the fairy-tale, dream-like quality of the piece and of the notion of love in the abstract.[28]

Whatever the views on male impersonation, it was generally considered that the role of Pelléas was rather insubstantial and not sufficiently testing for Sarah's powers: 'she simply smiled and warbled and languished through it. What else could she do?'[29] Mrs Patrick Campbell's recollections of Sarah in the role are more favourable, and she pinpoints the 'ecstasy and breeding' signified by her carriage and the 'voice of a youthful melancholy spirit, gradually melting into a tenderness, that more than once almost rendered me speechless for fear of breaking the spell'.[30] Miraculously, the two actresses with their wildly different, clashing personalities – Sarah dedicated to the pursuit of theatrical success, Mrs Pat ever the playful dilettante – managed to survive the play together. Not, it might be added, without playing a few tricks on each other: at one point Sarah filled the stage fountain – which Mrs Campbell had decried as a 'silly fishpond' – with awful-looking fish, catching the English actress unawares and causing her to choke back her laughter before she could speak her lines.[31] Despite its drawbacks, the enterprise had proved successful enough for Sarah and Mrs Campbell to revive it the following summer on a July tour of the provinces, following Sarah's June performances at the Coronet.

Sarah's interest in *travesti* continued until the close of her career. In 1905 she played Assuérus in Racine's *Esther*, staged by Sardou, which attempted to copy the original Saint-Cyr production designed for Louis XV and performed entirely by women. She recaptured the mood of *Pelléas et Mélisande* as the prince in the fairy-tale poetry of *La Belle au bois dormant* by Richepin and Henri Cain at the Théâtre Sarah Bernhardt in December 1907. Just as she had performed in a male lead opposite one of London's leading actresses, she undertook a similar enterprise in Paris. She played the poet to Julia Bartet's incarnation of the muse (which

Sarah had previously created at her theatre in 1900) in Musset's *La Nuit de Mai* in May 1909, on the occasion of Adeline Dudlay's retirement from the Comédie Française.[32] Several roles which she wanted to undertake as *travesti* performances were never realised. In her treatise on the theatre, she regrets not having played Goethe's Mephistopheles and Molière's Miser.[33] These remained in the planning stages, although the *Faust* production got as far as rehearsals early in 1908, only to be abandoned when Sarah and the adaptor of the piece, Henry Bataille, could not agree on cuts to the text.[34] Rumours of a Rostand *Faust* in progress also failed to materialise, though she did get to undertake Rostand's Cyrano in extract form (1909). During her American tour in 1916, she played Shylock in the trial scene of Shakespeare's *Merchant of Venice*. Moreover, for the New York performances of this tour, she alternated the role of Shylock with that of Portia, cross-dressing as a lawyer for the trial.[35]

It is to Sarah's credit that, towards the end of her life and career, she was still performing *travesti* roles or rather that she was able to perform at all, given that she was plagued by ill health. In particular she suffered increasingly from a pain in her leg which arose from an old wound sustained in one of her Tosca leaps and which had never been properly treated. By 1913 she was in considerable and constant pain, though this did not prevent her from continuing with full-length performances. However, she collapsed in the role of Marguerite during a Belgian tour in the May of 1914. Periods of rest were not enough, and in February 1915 her leg was amputated.

That this did not prevent Sarah from returning to the stage is testimony to that amazing will to live life to the full which had coloured her whole existence. She had no wish to be remembered as an ailing, handicapped, old woman but as a legendary and glamorous international star. Her courage and desire to spend the rest of her days in public, as opposed to the obscurity of retirement, meant that despite the amputation of her leg, she would add another, full-length, male impersonation to her repertoire. In November 1920 she appeared in Louis Verneuil's *Daniel* and found the energy to perform the role for a fortnight in London the following April.

The play, written by her grandson-in-law, is based on a domestic scenario in which Daniel, critically ill and addicted to morphine, is passionately in love with his brother's wife, Geneviève. When his distant adoration is shattered by the news that she has betrayed her husband for an old friend and is threatened with exposure and a duel between husband and lover, he saves them all by declaring himself to be her lover, though this act brings about his own death.

For the first two acts Sarah was not on stage, and this generated the feeling that in the beginning, 'proceedings had so far assumed something of the character of "Hamlet" without the Prince of Denmark'.[36] The play itself was generally disliked, but the occasion of Sarah's last performance in London was an occasion in itself, and the drama was irrelevant. It was Sarah that the glittering, first-night audience, which included ambassadors from the United States, France, Belgium and Japan, had come to see.

For the younger critics who had not been able to see Sarah in her heyday, there was a sufficient remnant of her former magnetism and the presence of a 'compelling personality' to indicate the greatness of the performer who came before them. Although Sarah had to remain seated, she captivated her audience by means of gesture and voice. She improved on an English version of the play which had been seen two or three months earlier at the St James's Theatre, which had had Daniel dying offstage, by offering her final, quiet and moving death scene, full of pathos and beauty. Admiration for her courage and acting was universal. 'There was the old fire in her acting', wrote the *Daily Telegraph*'s reviewer, 'the old magic in her voice, the old power to dominate the audience by her exquisite pathos or marvellous magnetism . . .That she should be able at 75 to sway people as she did is little short of a miracle'.[37]

That Sarah's English audiences did not enthuse as wildly over her *travesti* efforts as they did over her victim–heroine repertoire is only partly a reflection on Sarah's talent and ability; it is more predominantly coloured by their prejudicial attitude towards women and cross-dressing. Accustomed to the convention of *travesti*, her native audiences were not conditioned by the same prejudice, and yet they too preferred her female repertoire. The fact that Sarah's ventures into *travesti* roles never, with the exception of *L'Aiglon*, reached the heights of popularity attained by

Théodora or Tosca – were often polite successes or even failures – signifies the magnetic appeal of the 'sexed' actress in petticoats, over the 'unsexed' androgyny of her male guises.

## Notes

1. May Agate, *Madame Sarah*, p. 158.
2. See Dutton Cook, 'Ellen Terry', *Theatre*, June 1880, pp. 340–3.
3. Sarah Bernhardt, *L'Art du théâtre*, p. 141.
4. Ibid., p. 142.
5. Sarah Bernhardt, 'Men's Roles as Played by Women', *Harper's Bazaar*, 33 (15 December 1900), pp. 2113–5 (see p. 2115).
6. Gerda Taranow, *The Art within the Legend*, p. 217.
7. *Pall Mall Gazette*, 18 June 1897.
8. Kate Terry Gielgud, *A Victorian Playgoer* (London: Heinemann, 1980), p. 57.
9. *Daily News*, 18 June 1897.
10. *Star*, 18 June 1897.
11. *Pall Mall Gazette*, 25 October 1899.
12. *Daily Telegraph*, 12 June 1899.
13. *Era*, 17 June 1899.
14. Elizabeth Robins, 'On seeing Madame Bernhardt's Hamlet', *North American Review*, 171 (December 1900), pp. 908–19.
15. Max Beerbohm, *Around Theatres* (London: Rupert Hart Davis, 1953), p. 34.
16. Ibid., p. 37.
17. Sarah Bernhardt, *L'Art du théâtre*, p. 143.
18. John Hansen, 'Bernhardt as Hamlet', *National Magazine* (August 1899), pp. 469–72 (see p. 469).
19. Suze Rueff, *I Knew Sarah Bernhardt* (London: Frederick Muller, 1951), p. 78.
20. Elizabeth Robins, *North American Review*, p. 919.
21. *The Times*, 13 June 1899. Clement Scott's essay on Sarah's Hamlet is contained in his *Some Notable Hamlets* (New York & London: Benjamin Blom, 1969), pp. 43–51.
22. Sarah Bernhardt, *L'Art du théâtre*, p. 141.
23. *Daily Telegraph*, 4 June 1901.
24. *Star*, 4 June 1901.
25. *Daily Telegraph*, 18 June 1903.
26. Extract from the *Saturday Review*, reprinted by Margot Peters in *Mrs Pat* (London: Bodley Head, 1984 ), p. 250.

27. *Pall Mall Gazette*, 2 July 1904.
28. See *Daily News*, 2 July 1904.
29. *The Times*, 2 July 1904.
30. Mrs Patrick Campbell, *My Life and some Letters* (London: Hutchinson, 1922), p. 137.
31. See Suze Rueff, *I Knew Sarah Bernhardt* (London: Muller, 1951), p. 139.
32. For a description, see Ernest Pronier, *Sarah Bernhardt*, p. 128.
33. Sarah Bernhardt, *L' Art du théâtre*, p. 142.
34. See Ernest Pronier, *Sarah Bernhardt*, p. 126.
35. See Gerda Taranow, *The Art within the Legend*, pp. 216–7.
36. *Daily Telegraph*, 5 April 1921.
37. Ibid.

# 8 Conquering the Coliseum

Aside from Sarah's explorations of the *travesti* genre, the first decade of the new century saw her struggling to find further additions to her repertoire. As Roxane to Coquelin's Cyrano in the 1901 season, she sparkled and delighted but was eclipsed by the great French actor in the more substantial and varied role of the hero, compared to whom the romantic heroine is rather flimsy and insignificant. Similarly, the title role of *Francesca da Rimini* in the 1902 season failed to feed her dramatic appetite. Neither *Sapho*, nor *Plus que reine* the following season, generated any of the magnetism of her former triumphs. As Hermione in *Andromaque*, her classical addition to the 1903 season, she acquitted herself admirably but did not create the impression which she might have done, had she presented the tortured princess to her London audiences earlier in her career. Sardou's *La Sorcière* in 1904 did not redress this downward trend, being a thinly disguised melodrama with little flesh to cover the 'dry bones'.

Although these were lean years in terms of new roles, they were not a reflection on Sarah's own levels of enthusiasm and energy. Biographers cite her ability to maintain an exceptionally full working day, often rehearsing after an evening performance or sitting down to a midnight reading of a new play. Yet she was also a great socialite and always found time to entertain her wide circle of friends, both at home and abroad. In her own Théâtre Sarah Bernhardt, she had a suite of rooms designed both for her own comfort and for the reception and entertainment of guests. On her London visits, she entertained lavishly and extravagantly at whichever villa or hotel she was housed (often either the Savoy or the Carlton). So, while there were years in which her theatrical output seemed to have lost some of its brilliance, as in the early part of the new century, her life style remained as exacting, energetic and extravagant as it had ever been.

In 1905, Sarah achieved some of her former glory by reviving Hugo's prose drama, *Angelo, tyran de Padoue*, which she presented first at her own theatre in February and then brought to London to open her season of plays in June. As the courtesan–actress, La Tisbé, martyred in the name of unrequited love, Sarah was back in the world which suited her best. The Venetian setting, the intrigue, spies, poisonings and affairs of the heart enabled her to cajole and seduce, to fluctuate between jealous rage and womanly tenderness in a way which encircled the courtesan–sinner with a halo of saintliness. As to the play itself, the English critics of 1905 could find little to tempt the modern palate in a drama firmly entrenched in the Romantic conventions and concerns of the 1830s, thereby seriously questioning the rationale of its revival. Moreover, the dramatic action is shared by the evil, scheming spy, Homodei, the tyrannical Angelo, his wife Catarina – La Tisbé's rival in love – and the much sought after lover, Rodolfo. In short, the many protagonists caught in the tangled web radically reduced the amount of dramatic time and space that could be given over to the Bernhardtesque passion, which was generally regretted.

Faced with the problem of finding more suitable dramatic material, Sarah tried her own hand at playwrighting, in an attempt to create a leading role tailored to her own requirements. She produced her own version of Scribe and Legouvé's *Adrienne Lecouvreur*, which premièred in London on 27 June 1905 in her Coronet season, inaugurated by her role as La Tisbé. Prior to this six-act venture, Sarah had written only one, one-act play, *L'Aveu*, performed at the Odéon in 1888. In the latter she shows a focus of interest developed in *Adrienne Lecouvreur* and further explored in her four-act play which came afterwards – *Un Coeur d'homme* (1909), dedicated to Paul Hervieu – as all three centre on heroines in distress. *L'Aveu* depicts a domestic crisis in which a young mother is forced to admit that her baby son, on the brink of death, was not sired by her older husband but by the young doctor now caring for the baby. In *Adrienne Lecouvreur* the rewriting aims to highlight the heroine's thwarted love and the injustice of the tragic fate which befalls her. In *Un Coeur d'homme*, the heroine jumps to her death, à la Tosca, when her one moment of passion with her best friend's husband is discovered. None of these reveals any great literary merit. They merely take advantage of Sarah's understanding of the situations and character-types, which would best showcase tableaux of distressed heroines.

From Sardou she had learnt the value of dramatic irony, the thrill for the audience, who have full knowledge of the guilty secret, while the characters have only fragments. Her playwrighting echoes this school of melodramatic intrigue in which event piles on event, precipitating the inevitable climax of death or tragic despair.

English critics were divided over the merits of the new Adrienne – some preferred the original and wished she had left well enough alone; others enjoyed the violent, at times thrilling, clashes between Adrienne and her rival, the Duchess, which were stressed in the re-writing. In any event, the audience was hugely delighted, particularly with the encounter of the two rivals in act two, after which Adrienne sank exhausted into her lover's arms, and with the death scene, by which they were singularly moved. Yet all of this had much more to do with Sarah the actress, than Sarah the playwright.

Despite Sarah's endeavours to find a new direction in her work, her efforts were still in some sense found wanting and perhaps began to indicate a waning in her physical strength and well-being, the reality of her suffering, which would ultimately prove disabling, betraying the myth of perpetual youth. As Thérèse in Hervieu's *Le Réveil*, played at the Royalty in 1907 when Sarah was in her early sixties, she was a very subdued and quiet heroine, seizing none of the opportunities which the emotional conflict of the drama provided and demonstrating none of the sensational ingredient with which her London audiences associated her. The following years were even leaner, with Sardou dying in 1908, and no new playwrights coming forward with roles for the great actress. As Sarah left in 1908 for another, in fact, the last of her grand European tours taking her as far as Russia and then spent much of the summer in 1909 touring French provinces, one might have been forgiven for thinking that the heyday of her London years was well and truly over, and that she was effecting a gradual and graceful exit from the stage which had been her summer home for so many years.

All this was reversed in 1910, when Sarah embarked on the final phase of her English stage career, by beginning a new venture at one of London's finest music-halls, the Coliseum. Music-hall in England had come a long way since the mid-nineteenth-century pioneering days of Charles Morton's Canterbury Arms. The original rooms for music-halls, mere adjuncts to public houses, had given way to an architectural boom in the building of halls during 1880s, as the entertainment grew in popularity and proved a lucrative source of capitalist enterprise. With expansion came the incorporation of the respectable, wealthy middle classes into audiences which had been largely working-class in origin, and popular culture for the wealthy was epitomised in the elaborate and elegant venues of the Alhambra, the Tivoli and the Palace. The legal conflict that had existed throughout the second half of the nineteenth century between theatre and the halls over the sketch play gave way as the great actors and actresses were persuaded to appear in sketches in the top halls. The star syndrome of the legitimate stage, waning with the advent of the new, collective theatrical enterprises, found an alternative home and a new lease on life in the star turns of the halls, which enabled different kinds of artistes to contribute short, self-contained acts to the programme of entertainment. The Coliseum, which opened late in 1904, was managed by Oswald Stoll, who officiated over a whole chain of halls. As the 'Theatre de Luxe of London', the Coliseum attracted the finest and greatest performers from stage and variety, playing to capacity crowds of around 4,000 spectators.[1]

Sarah, as always, had need of an income to support her extravagant life style and family entourage. She had always to recoup the excessive losses of her overindulged and spendthrift son, whose artistic talent in no way measured up to his capacity for spending. As Maurice had married Thérèse Jablonowska (known as Terka) in 1887 and subsequently produced two daughters, Sarah's dependents had grown in number. Neither had her own desires for a luxurious style of living diminished. She still cultivated expensive tastes in costume, furnishings and accommodation (for herself, her family and her numerous and ever-increasing menagerie of exotic pets). Similarly, her sumptuous choice of theatrical costume and scenery all had to be paid for.

Consequently, as the only viable, independent wage-earner in her extended family, retirement was out of the question. Equally, her need to live out her days in a style befitting her international star status outweighed her fears of debasing her art by appearing on the same programme as variety acts and performing animals. In turn, her acceptance of Stoll's contract at the Coliseum would put her in touch with a hitherto undiscovered English public, whose class and culture kept them out of the theatres. When Sarah arrived in London to make her Coliseum début in the autumn of 1910, she was approaching her sixty-seventh birthday. Yet she retained an extraordinary vitality and youthfulness, which continued to astonish her reviewers. The English reviews from the music-hall years are coloured by expressions of frank incredulity over her youthful spirit and vigour, as Sarah continued to be as 'divine' as ever. She took the Coliseum by storm, appearing twice daily, afternoons and evenings, in extracts from *L'Aiglon* and *La Tosca*. When performing from her old repertoire, she chose acts which had most to offer in terms of visual and theatrical content, recognising that it was difficult to conquer her audiences now that the class range had widened, and the majority had no knowledge of French. Lack of familiarity with the plays was an additional disadvantage, audiences not knowing what had gone before and what was to come after the selected extract. A collection of plot synopses with detailed emphasis on the acts to be performed could be purchased for a few pence and helped to overcome some of the difficulty.

Although Sarah no longer faced the gruelling task of long evening performances, the twice-daily, thirty-minute turn had its own rigors, not least of which was trying to engage the audience in an appropriate mood for tragedy in the middle of a variety programme given over extensively to comic turns, rousing choruses and spectacular dancing. Yet Sarah, as ever when faced with a challenge, rose to meet it and proved herself more than equal to the demands made upon her. Amidst the laughter and hilarity of the surrounding acts, Sarah would hold her audiences spellbound and silent until the final moment, when the tension and hush of the packed auditorium was broken by thunderous applause.

Sarah's programme opened on Monday 19 September. As act number 12, she stepped forward as the boyish son of Napoleon. She chose the second act from *L'Aiglon*, in which the youth is seen resenting his confinement, fitfully bursting into moments of patriotism, dreaming lost dreams and reduced to campaigning with

135

his battlefield of toy soldiers. It was not an immediately accessible piece, although her graceful frailty and passionate outpouring of the Napoleonic spirit made a memorable impression:

The years, it is now a commonplace to say so, seem to have no power on Madame Bernhardt. She still bears herself a boy, and looks the boy triumphantly. The beautiful voice, is as beautiful as ever. At the note of command it peals out like a trumpet blast. The echo of 'je déchire' rings clear with the sad note of the tears of human things. Memories of days further back in life than we want to count are as yesterday while we watch *L'Aiglon*.[2]

As this review indicates, coupled with the reference to her boyish youth, was an increasing note of nostalgia. Sarah's style of theatre belonged to a past age, waning with the advent of the new, but for which she stood as a monument to and reminder of the great international days of star theatre.

Monday was the weekday on which the programme at the Coliseum changed, and on Monday 3 October after two weeks of *L'Aiglon*, Sarah switched from her duc de Reichstadt to the agonies of Tosca. The audience was greatly moved by Sarah's performance as the anguished heroine; though not being able to follow the words as such, the effect was achieved through the 'feeling' of the piece. Act three, the torture scene, which was the extract chosen, concludes with the recovery of Angelotti's body. Some advised that it would have made better theatrical sense to condense the end of the act, as no one was interested in this piece of stage business, and to have carried the action over into the killing of Scarpia, as the stabbing scene was both highly visual and sensational.[3] Nevertheless, Sarah's choice of extract was played to an enthusiastic crowd, who called the actress ten times at the end of her turn. M. Decoeur, who supported her as Scarpia (and as Flambeau in *L'Aiglon*), was admirably villanous and polarised the virtue of Tosca with a suitably evil behaviour, making the piece easily decodable in terms of melodrama-types, universally understood in any language.

Sarah's act was followed by another French artist, more at home in the halls than Sarah: Yvette Guilbert. Yvette's songs and sketches from the *cafés-concerts* had brought her international fame. In the past, she had not been averse to using the great

French actress as material for a parodic sketch or song.[4] That would have been too disrespectful on this occasion. Instead she entertained the audience with four or five songs, in French and English, particularly delighting everyone with 'Les Cloches de Nantes', which she accompanied with the swaying of her crinoline skirt in a bell-like fashion! A flavour of the cosmopolitan had clearly come to Stoll's Coliseum.

Encouraged by the overwhelming success of her first music-hall season, Sarah returned in the autumn of 1911 to revive three of her most popular roles in extract form and to offer one new interpretation. Of the old favourites, she offered act three of *Théodora*, with which she opened on 18 September, act three of *Fédora* (2 October), and for the final week the fifth act of *La Dame aux Camélias* (23 October). The new addition was act two from her second Joan of Arc: Moreau's *Le Procès de Jeanne d'Arc* (9 October). All four of these, in their several ways, focused on some aspect of the heroine subjected to torture.

When she opened in *Théodora* the Coliseum was packed with two generations of playgoers and plenty of young French people who had come to see Sarah – many spectators had to be turned away.[5] Her extract from Sardou's drama began with the Emperor's inquisition over his wife's nocturnal ramblings and reached its climax in the stabbing of the conspirator. There was nothing jaded about Sarah's performance. She was as brilliant and as thrilling as in her former years. As in 1879, critics now thirty years on attempted to demystify and analyse her magnetism:

Perhaps it is the authority of her acting that holds you wondering, her power of dominating scene and action and audience, even though the words she has to speak are altogether tinsel. You do not for a moment believe in the play, and yet the actress makes you believe in her. A triumph not of technical skill, not of imagination or subtlety, but of sheer personal force.[6]

How much was down to art and how much was accounted for by her star personality once more became an ongoing debate, and many reviewers, in the course of time, were prepared to modify their view from stardom to art. For audiences, the blaze of star publicity inevitably remained a large and significant factor.

Her snippet from *Fédora* contained those scenes in which the princess is tortured by the dawning knowledge of the misfortunes she has unwittingly heaped upon the head of her new lover. As the act begins with Ipanoff's long explanations, the opening was rather tedious for the audience who were unable to follow his wordy account of past events. The scene only came alive as Sarah communicated Fédora's fears through her body and facial gestures, in which language was not necessary, and brought events, at length, to a powerful climax.

This year, Sarah was supported by the young actor from Holland, Lou Tellegen – performer, writer and former pupil of the master sculptor, Rodin.[7] Rumours of a love affair were abroad, though these were hotly denied by Sarah, and seem rather incongruous given the disparity in their ages. He had a certain talent, sufficient at least for a supporting role, though there was never any danger of his youth and beauty eclipsing Sarah's commanding presence. As Armand to Sarah's Marguerite, he cut a particularly dashing figure. Critics were at a loss to find something new to say about the death scene of the courtesan, which they found as wonderful as ever – the *Daily Telegraph* going so far as to recommend Sarah's death scenes as 'essential study in any liberal theatrical education'.[8]

More reviewing space was given over in the theatre columns to the new Jeanne d'Arc. The second act dramatises the inquisition of Jeanne by the English Earls of Warwick, Winchester and Bedford on a charge of blasphemy. As Jeanne recites the story of her childhood, Sarah had plenty of scope for deploying the golden tones, crescendoing in the prophecy of the English expulsion from France seven years hence, when nothing – 'rien-rien-rien' – would remain of them. The heroine is threatened with physical torture, and a bag of instruments for breaking her fingers is produced to substantiate the threat. Fortunately, both Jeanne and the audience were spared this horror, as Bedford (Tellegen) intervened to prevent it, and the curtain fell on the unconscious maid, laid out on the table where she had been placed for torture. Powerful acting, familiarity with the Joan of Arc legend and a highly visual content ensured a successful reception. That Sarah spent time and thought on the stage management of her supporting players is indicated in the following description from *The Times*:

These sour ecclesiastics and harsh lawyers and savage English nobles form a half moon: and throughout the scene it seems as if the arc was narrowing and the horns coming closer and closer together till they all but meet round the tall, slim figure of Jeanne, who stands up, still in her coat-of-mail, and answers, with ever-rising emotion but with the same almost childish simplicity and confidence, the questions that are barked or snarled at her from this quarter or that and finally howled at her from all sides.[9]

Though Sarah dominated the scene, she took care to ensure that the setting and grouping of characters was appropriate and effective. Altogether, Sarah's 68-year-old Jeanne d'Arc had a far greater impact on her Coliseum audience than the younger Jeanne at Her Majesty's in 1890.

In the first week of the 1911 season, she was joined on the variety programme by two other stars – Albert Chevalier and Miss Cecilia Loftus, who had a long wait to come on for her impersonations after *Théodora*, as Sarah's curtain calls went on and on. During the *Fédora* run, one of the top acts was an illusionist who spirited a 'mermaid' into a tank of water, and in the last week, 'Talera', a *travesti* artiste, was practising something of Sarah's art, only this time the lady turned out to be a man. Although the programme was given over mainly to comedians and artistes of the halls, Sarah was by no means the only professional actress playing in music-hall. While she was enthralling the Coliseum audience with her tortured heroines, Réjane was playing an extract from Sardou's *Mme Sans Gêne* at the Hippodrome. 'High Art' had rapidly become a popular feature of mass culture.

Spurred on by the success of her Jeanne d'Arc, Sarah offered more new roles in 1912. She opened on Monday 16 September for two weeks as Hugo's Lucrèce Borgia. Twice a day, at 4:15 and 9:45, she appeared as the villainess. The play had proved surprisingly successful when the full-length version had been revived by Sarah at her theatre in November 1911. With regard to the extract, English critics were far more impressed by the actress than the play which, like *Angèlo*, they viewed as far less important to audiences of the 1900s than to the Romantics of the 1830s. The piece which Sarah selected for her thirty-minute turn shows Lucrèce struggling between a mother's love and her fiendish nature, as she has brought upon herself a situation in which she is forced to poison her illegitimate son, whom her husband, the Duke, believes to be her lover. Once the poison is administered and Lucrèce is left alone with her 'lover' to see him die, she cajoles him into drinking an antidote.

The performance received enthusiastic reviews from the critics, notably on two counts – Sarah's portrayal of the conflicting interests of the maternal and the fiendish and her vocal dexterity in the part. As the extract was highly charged with violent emotion and theatrical incident, Sarah had every opportunity 'to play on most of the strings of the "lyre" . . . passionate emotion, haughty defiance, harrassed agony, despair, wrath, and finally exultation, to fully express each and all she was equal, and showed no falling off of force and power'.[10] She moved, as the *Daily Telegraph* reviewer described, '*du pathètique tendre au pathètique terrible*', always the queen, and yet always 'a woman, with all a woman's arts of pleading and caress and appeal at her will'.[11]

Her use of voice in the Coliseum had been commonly remarked upon, both this year and last. It required great vocal dexterity to fill the vast and formidable auditorium without falling foul of the echo, as May Agate describes in her reminiscences of Sarah's 1912 season, in which she took part.[12] Whether Sarah was the frail Jeanne d' Arc or the scheming Lucrèce, her voice filled the huge auditorium. She carefully articulated her lines in French so that those who, with a little understanding of the language, might be able to follow could do so: 'her smooth staccato voice . . . accents every syllable so that her French can be followed by the schoolgirl – and the schoolgirl's mother – who will fill the Coliseum during the next few weeks'.[13]

After Lucrèce came a revival of her Phèdre, partnered by Tellegen's Hippolyte. Sarah took up the action at the end of act one, as Phèdre reveals her guilty secret to her *confidente*, and climaxed with the tempestuous encounter with Hippolyte in act two. Her enactment of the distress of a noble nature overcome by a shameful and uncontrollable passion was as vivid and electric as that of over thirty years ago, and the music-hall audience were treated to a pleasurable instruction in French verse by means of Sarah's excellent delivery:

No one of our time finds such richness, such variety of beauty in the cold French verse as she. On her lips it becomes infinitely flexible, capable of all the emotions of the heart. She gives the glow of life to its measured grace, and a richer deeper music to it, be it the fever of shame, the devices of the tortured soul to free itself, or the wild demand of passion, it is invested with beauty. All is real enough, and terribly real, but it all has a nobility of soul. This is the true grandeur of 'the grand style'.[14]

However, it would also be true to say that, whereas the drama critics still looked to the delivery, style and artistic content of Sarah's performance and paid scant attention to the music-hall context, a large proportion of her less discerning audience would have been drawn simply by the idea of seeing Sarah Bernhardt, the legendary star. From this point of view, Sarah was as much a novelty as the conjuring, juggling or comedy acts featured on the same bill.

After the tragedy of the French queen, came the dying moments of Moreau's *Elisabeth, Reine d'Angleterre*, which Sarah played for two weeks, opening on 7 October. Having sat patiently in the past through the dramatisation of chapters from French history – the Saint Joans and the Eaglets – it seemed only fair that her adoring English audiences should be rewarded by a chapter from their own. She had Adelaide Ristori's earlier nineteenth-century success in the role of Elisabeth – her most frequently performed part – as an indicator of the English queen's dramatic potential. Sarah performed the role in its entirety at the Théâtre Sarah Bernhardt in April 1912 and then offered the final act at the Coliseum on a programme which also included bioscope pictures of Captain Scott's Antarctic expedition.

Elisabeth, in her final hour, is seen as a lonely, tragic figure afraid of death. She is haunted by remorse for her former treatment of Mary Queen of Scots and Essex, only now discovering that Essex had in fact sent her the ring – the token which would have saved him from execution – but that it had been intercepted by Lord Howard. The revelation takes her nearer to death. Sarah showed both sides of the character, the queen and the woman, each with their public and private laments – the queen for her kingdom without an heir, which must of necessity pass to James of Scotland, and the woman bitterly resenting her thwarted love.

141

As Lady Lucy, who reveals the tragedy of the ring, May Agate made her début on the English stage with her French mentor. She describes how her first night was spent resisting the laughter which had convulsed the Elisabethan courtiers, when she was announced as Lord and not Lady Lucy.[15] Sarah alone resisted the general hilarity, though she was not averse to a joke herself, and Agate recalls one performance night 'when there was a good deal of coughing, and Madame Sarah, knowing the bulk of the audience didn't seize every phrase, said, fairly loud up, in accents of dire grief, "Ils toussent! Donnez-leur donc à boire!" lifting a silver goblet to her dying lips'.[16]

As a contrast to this succession of guilt-ridden, remorseful, regal figures, Sarah presented the one-act play, *Une Nuit de Noël sous la Terreur*, by Maurice Bernhardt and Henri Cain, for the last week of her season (21 October). The play is set in a farmhouse in La Vendée, in the days of the Revolution, Sarah taking the role of the *vivandière* who saves a family of aristocrats by making a passionate appeal to the military liberators to spare them. The piece itself was of little consequence, but it provided Sarah with the opportunity of 'humour in the first part', in which she made her entrance coming out of a snowstorm in a donkey cart, and 'womanly tenderness and tragic earnestness in the second'.[17] The one-act structure of a self-contained piece facilitated comprehension, and its simple and direct royalist message had an immediate appeal for the English audience. The house, as crowded as ever for Bernhardt's performances – young girls 'perched on the back partition' to the rear of the royal circle, 'steadied by the arms of their companions' – was hugely delighted by this final spectacle.[18]

On the 23 October, celebrations for Sarah's sixty-eighth birthday were held at the Savoy Hotel. Dignitaries and leading members of the acting profession gathered together to pay tribute to the great French actress, who had been appearing on the English stage for over thirty years. Lady Bancroft presented her with an address signed by approximately 100,000 well-wishing admirers. Sir Herbert Tree, Earl Beauchamp and the French Ambassador Paul Cambron made speeches in her honour, the latter recalling Sarah's first major triumph, *Le Passant*, from the Odéon years. In return, Sarah's speech of thanks, for once spoken in English, praised the London audiences which had welcomed her over the years, expressing the hope that through her art she had contributed in a small way to the *Entente Cordiale*. She concluded with a thrilling and memorable plea, after the fashion of one of her stage heroines, for the continued unity of 'the two noblest passions of life, *L' Art et la Patrie*'.

When Sarah returned to England in 1913, it was without the support of Tellegen, who had decided to break away and risk his fortunes on the American stage. It was not an irreparable loss, as his presence on stage was determined by physical beauty rather than acting talent, and the gap he left was now filled by M. Joube. In the autumn of 1913, Joube played Justinien to her Théodora, Armand to her Marguerite, was Bedford alongside her Jeanne, and played the unfortunate count saved by Sarah's *vivandière*. To these were added two new pieces: act two of Rostand's *La Samaritaine* and another one-act play by Henri Cain and Maurice Bernhardt, *La Mort de Cléopâtre*.

Rostand's *La Samaritaine* belonged to Sarah's Renaissance repertoire (April 1897), but she had not played it in England because of the censorship regarding the portrayal of biblical characters on the stage. Now that these laws had relaxed, Sarah seized the opportunity to revive her 'Woman of Samaria'. In an interview with the *Morning Post*, she described how she had carefully avoided those scenes which require the presence of Christ and the Apostles, opting instead for the scenes from act two, in which Photine returns to her village to recount her meeting with Jesus at the well and to spread the word of his teaching.[19] Her news is discredited, first by her lover, friends, priests and then, ironically, by the Roman centurion (Joube), who is sent to arrest her for causing a disturbance, but lets her go, feeling convinced of her insignificance. Photine belongs to the Magdalen-type of repentant sinner, and Sarah had an appropriate vehicle for her womanliness and winning ways, as she cajoled and worried the crowd into finally taking her part. Likewise her melodious delivery of Rostand's verse won over the Coliseum crowd, and there was nothing in the extract that could be possibly construed as irreverent or likely to cause offence.

*La Samaritaine* opened the first week of the season (8 September), *La Mort de Cléopâtre* brought it to a close (13–18 October),

143

the familiar extracts coming in between. Cain and Bernhardt's Cléopâtre was the Sardou queen in miniature and included both the stabbing of an Egyptian dignitary who has designs upon her person and the triumph over Caesar as the queen takes control over her regal and dignified death. The emphasis on death scenes in the Coliseum seasons is indicative both of Sarah's own desire for acting death in a grand manner and their epitome of all that was commonly recognised as Bernhardtesque.

The increasing respectability of music-hall was signified that year by the occasion of a charity night, attended by the King and Queen on Saturday October 11, at which Bernhardt was the star attraction. The Coliseum was decked out in gold for the event: the tunnel entrance in Chandos St was transformed into a 'Royal Boudoir'; the auditorium was festooned with golden leaves and the royal box hung in gold drapery, all of which remained in place for the following week of Sarah's Cléopâtre performances. The proceedings were inaugurated by Ellen Terry, reading a verse prologue in tribute to Sarah. The first half of the pro-gramme was dominated by comedy and included W.C. Fields, Yvette Guilbert and the Humpsti-Bumpsti duo. In the second half the tone changed. Two Elgar marches preceded Sarah's Phèdre, which she played brilliantly, no doubt inspired by the occasion and the presence of royalty, and she received the great-est ovation of the evening.

The English public, unlike the French, had never proved slow to pay tribute to the actress at performances on public occasions, ceremonies, banquets in her honour and birthday salutes. Now at last, she received late recognition from her compatriots and was awarded the Legion of Honour at the close of 1913. Yet triumph was soon to be followed by tragedy as the suffering caused by her ailing leg – suffering which was all too visible during the 1913 Coliseum season – would not abate. After the subsequent ampu-tation in 1915, messages of sympathy flooded in from all over the world, and leading members of the English theatre were among the many who rushed to offer their condolences. Sarah's own tragedy seemed to personify the atrocities of war which were taking place everywhere. Ellen Terry, who at first could not believe the fate which had befallen her fellow actress, wrote as follows in her diary:

One thing I swear: Sarah *has not lost her soul*, and I love every bit of her that is left. I suppose it really is loss of rhythm, of balance, that makes *grotesque*. War is grotesque . . . I see D'Annunzio opens a verse campaign to speed the War. Well, the pen is mightier than the sword, and so the verse may cut deeper, and live on and cut for ever.[20]

Certainly Sarah shared in the belief that the war could be won with the help of art, and before long she was back in the theatre and on the battle fronts, where she was transported around in a specially designed chair, spreading her message of '*L'Art et la Patrie*'. To be active again was also the hallmark of a personal triumph over adversity and one which showed the reality of the fierce spirit beneath the legend, a spirit which refused, whether out of courage, pride or vanity, to retreat into a private and pitiable state of dependence.

At her Coliseum appearances during the war years, Sarah offered short pieces which were dramatised poems rather than plays and were designed to inspire patriotism. In January 1916, she appeared in *Les Cathédrales*, in which a French soldier is discovered asleep, dreaming of the great cathedrals of France, which take on animated form and speak to him of the sufferings of the nation, building up to a climactic call to arms. This dramatic poem by Eugène Morand was visually impressive. The six cathedrals were personified by actresses seated in stone-coloured chairs, their figures draped in grey and white garments. The set, shrouded in mist, cleared to reveal the seventh cathedral, Strasbourg, personified by Sarah, who was seated behind the others, slightly apart from them, and clad in classical robes. As a speaking picture, it relied essentially on Sarah's vocal power. Backed by the appropriately tragic tones of Gabriel Poré's music, her voice rang out with a cry for her suffering nation. When at the close she raised herself up for the Marseillaise and interpreted the anthem with gesture, she electrified the house.

To *Les Cathédrales* she added a patriotic piece of her own, *Du Théâtre au Champ d'Honneur*, in which she played a French soldier mortally wounded in the leg and chest, who insists on the recovery of his lost flag before death. Sarah was thus able to perform lying down and signified, through the sufferings of her own body and the acting of the part, the pathos of trench warfare. She created two opportunities for her golden voice, in the decla-

145

mation of 'The prayer for our enemies', beginning 'Father forgive them not, for they know what they do', and in verses from Paul Déroulède's poem, 'Au Porte-drapeau'. Both of these were deeply moving: 'Mme. Bernhardt put into the recital of the poem all the dramatic intensity of which she is master, and at times the scorn in her voice reproduced the crackle and sparkle of a burning bush', wrote one critic.[21] In her battle cry 'deeper and holier notes are sounding, and the golden voice brings to you the glory and courage and faith and honour and untimely death for the soul of France', wrote another.[22] While the remainder of the variety programme was given over to more cheerful comedy or farce routines, designed to relieve the despondency of war or, alternatively, to the rousing, jingoistic, military impersonations of Vesta Tilley, aimed likewise at rallying the British troops and nation, Sarah's acts made a far greater impression with their nobility and pathos.

Sarah's granddaughter, Lysiane, provided her with another wartime tableau, *Une d'elles*, which Sarah played with *Les Cathédrales* at the Coliseum in April 1916. It depicts the grief of a mother, who believing her elder son to be dead, dies herself through her suffering. It was a badly written piece, but given the current climate of adversity, the personification of a mother's grief over her son could not fail to move the audience to tears. Again, the beauty of the spoken tableau lay in Sarah's voice and her manner of dying: 'The beautifully modulated voice running on, every syllable of every word clear-cut as a cameo, in lamentation, beseeching, protest, prayer, resignation. And then the tranquil dying in the high-backed chair, the large eyes wide open, the mouth half-smiling'.[23]

Sarah's years at the Coliseum had shown the way in which the gap between art and culture might be bridged. By bringing Racine, Hugo, Dumas *fils* and many other lesser playwrights to the Coliseum, she had brought drama to many for whom theatre was a closed book. She succeeded in popularising the classics, and her art was a lesson for those who wished to see more people going to watch Shakespeare plays and other masterpieces. As one reviewer wrote in 1913, 'the kind of acting and of verse delivery which are necessary to make popular the classic drama of a nation may be seen and heard just now at the Coliseum, where

Sarah Bernhardt, at an unmentionable age, is drawing great crowds to listen to verse they don't understand, but of which they can hear every syllable; and detect every modulation'.[24] Even when handicapped by her physical disability, her voice went on magnetically drawing in the crowds, as she wielded her irresistible weapons of art and patriotism.

## Notes

1. For further details see Victor Glasstone, *Victorian and Edwardian Theatres* (London: Thames & Hudson, 1975), pp. 116–17.
2. *Daily Telegraph*, 20 September 1910.
3. See *Morning Post*, 4 October 1910.
4. For examples see Gerda Taranow, *Sarah Bernhardt*, pp. 59-60, p. 63 and p. 107.
5. Details in *Westminster Gazette*, 19 September 1911.
6. *Daily Telegraph*, 19 September 1911.
7. For further biographical details see Tellegen's interview with the *Era*, 12 October 1912.
8. *Daily Telegraph*, 24 October 1911.
9. *The Times*, 10 October 1911.
10. *Era*, 21 September 1912.
11. *Daily Telegraph*, 17 September 1912.
12. May Agate, *Madame Sarah*, p. 193.
13. *Star*, 17 September 1912.
14. *Daily Telegraph*, 1 October 1912.
15. May Agate, *Madame Sarah*, pp. 191–2.
16. Ibid., p. 192.
17. *Pall Mall Gazette*, 22 October 1912.
18. *Morning Post*, 22 October 1912.
19. *Morning Post*, 8 September 1913.
20. Ellen Terry, *Memoirs*, p. 295.
21. *Westminster Gazette*, 18 January 1916.
22. *Daily Telegraph*, 18 January 1916.
23. *Era*, 12 April 1916.
24. *Star*, 7 October 1913.

# 9 Quand Même

Sarah's final years saw her, once again, overtaken by wanderlust. Her disability, the pain and suffering it left her with, the recurring attacks of uremia as the poison in her blood ravaged her body, did not prevent her from living out her days in that grand style to which she had become accustomed and which was part of her legendary image. She crossed the seas to America in the autumn of 1916, playing throughout Canada and the United States with a small company, on a farewell tour. She did not return to France until 1918, when she disembarked at Le Havre on the day of the Armistice. The time of rejoicing was also a time of sadness for Sarah, as one by one, lifelong friends were disappearing from her world, her poet–dramatist, Edmond Rostand, for instance, dying shortly after her return to France.

In terms of her stage career, Sarah faced the problem of what to perform, given that for any part she undertook she had to be seated or supported by strategically placed props. For several months she confined herself to giving readings and recitals, which she toured around the French provinces and Europe, concentrating on extracts from verse drama which served to highlight her elocutionary skills. The motto she had adopted for her own – *Quand Même* – had greater significance than ever, as Sarah struggled on against the odds. Eventually she began to explore the possibility of performing roles which could be worked around her immobility. In January 1920, she appeared in *Rossini* at Lyons, playing the composer's mother. Biographical plays were in vogue after the Great War,[1] and Sarah scored a significant success in *Rossini*, which renewed her courage for a Parisian comeback, planned for Easter 1920, when she had arranged to appear in Racine's biblical drama *Athalie*. Sarah had calculated that the staging could be adapted to overcome her disability, and as Athalie only appears in two acts, the arduousness of undertaking a full-length role was mitigated. The occasion was a triumph for Sarah, and she need not have worried over the prospect of advancing years and infirmity resulting in a disappointing or embarrassing tableau. Suze Rueff describes how the Parisians rushed to see her, bringing with them their children and grandchildren, 'so that one day they too might be able to say they had heard and seen the great Sarah'.[2]

Just as in former years playwrights had designed roles and dramas which would best suit Sarah's talents, friends now offered her specially written pieces which worked around her disability – *Daniel*, her last male impersonation and last English performance, being one of these. In addition to *Daniel*, Verneuil created *Régine Armand* (April 1922), in which Sarah, as the tragedienne Régine, played her 'double'. While from the pen of Maurice Rostand, Edmond's son, whom Sarah indulged in memory of his father and who was fanatically devoted to Sarah, came *La Gloire* (October 1921) and *La Mort de Molière* (April 1922). Like his father, he wrote in verse and created allegorical figures for Sarah in both of these pieces – La Gloire and La Douleur respectively. A third piece written for her by Maurice, *Le Secret du Sphinx*, was never played by Sarah. She died before it went into rehearsal, and it was eventually performed by Sarah's pupil, Ida Rubinstein.[3]

There was no love lost between Verneuil and Rostand. As *La Gloire* was postponed so that Sarah might play *Daniel* first, Maurice Rostand was understandably put out. As a champion of French verse and theatre as 'high art', he detested Verneuil's inadequate and inept compositions (not that his own escaped similar criticism). There seems to have been deep personal animosity between them, and in his recollections of Sarah, Rostand expresses great relief over the failure of Verneuil's marriage to Sarah's granddaughter, Lysiane.[4]

As for Sarah, her maturity placed her above and beyond the petty squabbling which in former years would have inflamed her explosive artistic temperament. Descriptions of Sarah in these last years highlight her stoical and placid demeanour in the face of suffering and her mortality. The photographs taken shortly before her death are characterised by a spirit of 'otherness', the far-away look of her poetical, otherworldly stage princesses. Even so, she was always planning new projects and was always on the move.

Her final venture was the filming of *La Voyante*. Sarah was not unfamiliar with film cameras; several extracts from her theatre

149

had been recorded on film; the cameras had been invited into her home on Belle-Isle; and she had made a propaganda film in wartime, *Les Mères françaises*.[5] *La Voyante* had to be filmed at Sarah's home in the Boulevard Pereire as she was too ill to move. The photograph of her in the role of clairvoyant highlights her ashen, death-like pallor and haunted dark eyes.[6] She died without completing the film on 26 March 1923. Thousands crowded to her death bed to see her for one last time, laid out in a white robe, festooned with floral tributes. On the day of the funeral the people of Paris turned out to lay the great actress to rest:

> They lined the streets ten deep, all along the Boulevard Malesherbes, the Rue Royale, Rue de Rivoli, filling every window, every nook and vantage point, and overflowing on to the steps of palaces and churches along the route. Six coaches, draped in black, carried the flowers, to which more and still more were added on the way, and when the convoy halted for some minutes outside the Théâtre Sarah Bernhardt, a rain of flowers descended on to the coffin. Old men and women, some the artisans and midinettes of long ago, who so many times had waited in the queue for her first nights, openly wept, and many knelt in the street. For Sarah, the enchantress, had deserved well of them.[7]

She was buried in the Père Lachaise Cemetery, with a single-word inscription on her tombstone – 'BERNHARDT'.

In London, her passing was marked by a Requiem Mass held in Westminster Cathedral, attended by leading members of the acting profession, including her contemporary, Ellen Terry. Ellen was not long in following Sarah, dying in July 1928, though outliving Sarah's great rival, Duse, who died shortly after Sarah in 1924. It was the end of an era, the end of the great international actress and the global celebrity of the star performer, a phenomenon which, as Sarah possibly foresaw, was to re-emerge in the screen goddesses of the film industry.

Trying to offer a final summative overview of Sarah and her career on the English stage is a daunting and perhaps impossible task. As reviewers in her lifetime discovered, there was always something about the Bernhardtesque which appeared beyond the language of analysis or description and which makes the second-hand deconstruction and reconstruction of her work so difficult. It is hard not to fall into the trap of clichéd praise and amazement over a woman whose career was precisely that – amazing. However, to begin with the woman. Writing on Réjane's performance in *Zaza*, Arthur Symonds describes how the heroine was so completely different to Réjane's own character, and raises the question, 'What is the self of a great actress?'[8] Addressing this general question to Sarah in particular raises the issue of whether the private 'self' within the public performer is in any sense 'knowable'. Biographers from Sarah's circle of family, friends and artists have given their appraisals titles which imply an unequivocal sense of knowing – *I Knew Sarah Bernhardt* or *Sarah Bernhardt as I Knew Her*. The inclusion of the authorial 'I' is significant in so far as it reflects the egotistical nature of much of this biographical writing, the rush to stake a claim in having been privileged to number amongst her intimates. In fact, in the majority of cases these biographies are highly subjective versions of the 'truth', refractions of the Bernhardt myth according to a particular family or personal prejudice. Insights into the life of the private woman are hard, if not impossible, to find in such biographical documentation, which remains in the realms of myth-making and uncritical adulation.

In her own writing, Sarah is equally guilty of hiding behind a public mask. Her autobiography *Ma Double vie* implies the separation of actress and woman, but the writing, though reflecting the spirit of the age, is a fabrication of how Sarah wanted the public to see her, rather than the 'real' self within the legend. In interviews for magazines and newspapers she fabricated and fictionalised her life at will. She would please herself as to how she furthered or denied the stories (mostly of a romantic nature) circulated in the gossip columns. She helped to spread and to counter, for instance, the rumours of her recipe for the elixir of youth – attributed to a diet of shrimps, raw eggs and champagne![9] Her novel, *Petite idole* (1920), written to occupy her less active years of decline, epitomises this fictional approach, as it blends her own youthful experiences of theatre with those of the young actress-heroine, Espérance Darbois.[10] Yet although she would often allow gossip and scandal-mongering in the press to go unchecked, if her art or patriotism were called into question,

151

then she would retaliate with an unequivocal statement in defence.

She had a so-called 'private' life on her island, Belle-Isle, off the Brittany coast, where she retreated for some of the summer months when she was not performing. Yet even here, she had an entourage of family and friends – less numerous than in her Parisian studios and salons, but still a small audience. Reynaldo Hahn describes his arrival on the island, for instance, when he was greeted by 'Sarah, muffled in green gauze and wearing suede gloves, Suzanne Seylor, Mme Hammacher, Clairin, wearing a large straw hat trimmed with a long veil (why?), the elderly Geoffroy, Maurice with his wife and daughters surrounding me with their attentions'.[11] With such a personal entourage, and the presence of intrusive tourists trying to catch a glimpse of Sarah, any notion of 'private' or 'privacy' is wholly relative to the grand scale of her city or itinerant life style.

In her last years, when she lived more quietly, she was generally accompanied by her granddaughter Lysiane. Biographers comment on how she saw in Lysiane a reflection of her former, youthful self. Her refusal to acknowledge the reality of her aging body, preferring cosmetic disguises to maintain the illusion of the Bernhardtesque beauty, was a clear case of self-deception. The grey hair was concealed by a variety of artificial coiffures. The face was heavily caked with make-up; the eyes and lips accentuated in a grotesque travesty of youth – the familiar signs of the aging star, to whom only the distance between the performer and spectator is kind. Her interest in the *travesti* genre highlights her refusal to accept the aging process, as it enabled her to disguise the age of the woman in an image of adolescent androgyny.

The photographs and portraits of Sarah taken and painted throughout her life show how she wished to be seen and remembered. They capture the pictorial essence of her performance style: the distressed Phèdre, for example, gazing towards heaven and supported by her maid-servants, or Théodora, arms outstretched barring the way to her lover, are testimony to the emotionalist style she wished to immortalise. By virtue of their decorative, spiritual and mythical traits, Alphonse Mucha's publicity posters for Sarah's productions signify her literary and poetical aspirations. The style of the art work and the representations of Sarah denote a haloed and hallowed heroine, belonging to the Arthurian world of romance. Photographs and sketches of scenes from productions record Sarah's vision of the theatre as an *opéra parlé*, the huge casts grouped around Sarah captured in poses which externalised the inner emotions of the heroine. *Izéyl*, probably the first of Sarah's productions to be recorded by flash photography,[12] is documented, for example, by a series of photographs which show, tableau by tableau, the arabesque gestures of the heroine's decline, set against a background of numerous supporting figures.[13]

It becomes increasingly obvious as one sifts through biographies, reviews, photographs and films, that to separate the woman from the actress is impossible. In some crucial sense, Sarah refused to be 'known'. By deliberately courting an extravagant life style, fit to rival the excesses of her Byzantine Théodora, she encouraged the glamour of her stardom to conceal the qualities behind it: her tremendous will to succeed, her strength of independence, her sheer energy for living, and enormous courage in the face of adversity. These are lost in the representation of her star image, which encouraged extremes, of both adulation and criticism, but never with a sense of the 'real' Sarah. The 'self' of the great actress, to answer Symond's question, is wholly disguised by Sarah's public self-presentation, and until such time as private, reliable correspondence should come to light (if ever), then it is perhaps only through an analysis of her theatrical contribution that Sarah is 'knowable', a unified sense of her image at best conveyed through the polymorphous voices of her many heroines.

In order to present an overview of the contribution she made to the English stage, there are various aspects of her work which need to be taken into account. First and foremost is her style; her emotionalist method was incomparable. As Sarah made London her summer home, frequently supplemented by tours of the provinces, the English stage was privileged to witness an actress of consummate skill and talent. Whenever interviewed (as was often the case on her English visits) she was quick to defend her histrionic method, a defence she made throughout her career, and notably in the main, retrospective self-justification of her art, *L'Art du théâtre*. It is clear that even in terms of performance style, Sarah pursued her strategies of myth-making, as the omission of any analytical commentary on the divorce between theory and practice indicates. Yet clearly, as Gerda Taranow has demonstrated in her deconstruction of 'art' and 'legend',[14] Sarah did rely frequently on technique. The overall impression for the spectator, however, was one of sensibility, rather than a mannered style, à la Bartet or Hading, and therein lay the enormity of her success with English audiences. Her spell-binding tableaux of distraught or dying heroines, with whom she seemed as one, appealed to the current taste for larger-than-life spectacles of anguish which her grand style courted, indeed celebrated. There was an incredible vogue in Edwardian theatre for drama which moved the audiences to tears, and Sarah could do this better than anyone. It is unrealistic to think that she felt and cried as her character night after night without recourse to technique, as her theoretical writing would have us believe. Yet, however she induced her tears, it is certain that they were as real as the spectators' as they wept copiously into their handkerchiefs at the death of Marguerite or Froufrou. The Coliseum performances bear this out, as the music-hall audiences relied more heavily on tone, gesture and the feeling of the piece than on language. Hearts went out to the tortured heroines, not because they were won over by wordy debate, but because the *feeling* of distress was ably communicated by tone, face and body, all of which were invested with such force and passion that an audience were as carried away as the ill-fated figure represented before them.

English criticism and reviewing of her style centred on an analysis of gesture and voice. Sarah's combination of the Classical and the Boulevard, bringing together the statuesque and the pantomimic, resulted in a highly pictorial method in which inner emotions were externalised in poses signifying the passage through grief, jealousy, love, passion, seduction, and so forth. Much of her pathos was drawn from this method of picture-acting: Jeanne d'Arc on her knees begging for mercy, Marguerite, Fédora or Adrienne falling lifeless into the arms of their lovers. She used every part of her body to create the highly memorable effect she desired: the sorrowful gaze of her ethereal princesses, the serpentine undulations of her Egyptian queen, the agitation of the distressed Phèdre with her trembling fingertips, or the fluttering gestures of Fédora's hands in her moment of anagnorisis. What she communicated to spectators, critics and aspiring actresses was the power of her emotional method. The imitators of her style on the English stage, such as Modjeska or Mrs Bernard-Beere, had an excellent blueprint from which to work. The legacy of her acting method was formalised in later years, when she offered structured teaching to pupils at her own theatre, among whom at least one English actress, May Agate, was privileged to number.[15]

The magnetism of Sarah's 'golden voice' was constantly and continuously remarked upon from the start to the finish of her London career. Critics were reminded of its musical and lyrical quality when it was harshened for the purpose of the *travesti* roles. Its siren-like quality is substantiated in later years when, deprived of movement, she could still hold an audience spellbound by voice alone. Sarah's vocal abilities alerted the English critics to the lack of voice and speech training for their own actors and actresses, especially when Sarah proved she could popularise the verse-classics in music-hall.

The issue of voice training was only part of a larger concern in England for the lack of formal training for the stage and the absence of a national theatre. France had the Conservatoire and the Comédie Française. England had an *ad hoc* system of theatrical families, beauty queens with financial resources and society connections, and 'bit' part training with companies of actor-managers. When Matthew Arnold saw Sarah on the occasion of her first London visit with the Comédie in 1879, he saw in her the way to awaken interest in the theatre, in order to set about 'organising' it to a higher artistic aim.

With the need for training and a national theatre went the need for encouraging new playwrights. The lack of English playwriting was evident in the number of French plays on the nineteenth-century London stage, either performed in the original by visiting companies or presented in the form of English translations or adaptations. Critics were quick to criticise the verbosity of Dumas *fils*, the monotony of Rostand's verse or the melodrama of Sardou, but at least France had playwrights to criticise and,

155

moreover, playwrights who wrote chiefly about the subject dearest to the heart of Victorian and Edwardian audiences – romance and passion. It was internationally recognised that the French, for the time being at least, had cornered the market on passion, as evinced by Duse's difficulty in finding suitable Italian virtuoso roles to perform.

Among the modern French plays Sarah performed in London, Sardou's were unmistakable favourites. One does not have to probe deeply to understand why. Their pictorial and theatrical quality rendered them easily accessible and comprehensible. Where speech was prioritised over action, as in the case of Rostand's verse drama, it was harder, even with Sarah's excellent delivery, for English audiences to remain interested. Dumas's debating technique posed similar problems, especially when his dramatic thesis centred on marital questions peculiar to France, such as the 'Tue-la' doctrine. *La Dame aux Camélias* is the one exception; Dumas's formula of the saintly sinner evokes precisely the blend of pathos and passion which the audiences craved.

Given that Sarah's theatre drew on all its available resources – music, settings, costume, scenery, huge casts, etc. – it was a veritable feast of spectacle. Little has been said about Sarah in a directorial, managerial capacity, though clearly the reviews of the London productions point towards a firm grasp of stage-craft and an understanding of what would or would not work theatrically. Nevertheless, as a stage manager Sarah often stumbled across difficulties when transporting a production from her own theatre to one of the many London theatres in which she performed. Although she established Maurice in management at the Ambigu and went on to manage the Porte Saint-Martin, the Renaissance and finally the Nations, renamed the Théâtre Sarah Bernhardt, there was little continuity in her directorial work in the Parisian theatres as actress-manager, because of the international tours. Although plays were mounted without her, these were never significant enough to rival the absent figurehead. Nevertheless, Sarah used the theatres she managed to experiment with productions before they went on tour. This is verified by English critics who saw both Paris and London premières and who were able to comment on changes and amendments.

Duquesnel and Sardou were both instrumental in advising her

on matters of staging,[16] and the number of artists, musicians and writers among her acquaintances brought her into contact with the latest literary and artistic movements, enriching her understanding of stage-craft. Over the years she accumulated a thorough working knowledge of the theatre and was able to organise the acting space and her performers wherever she went. It is clear from the reviews of her London productions that Sarah did not simply help herself to the limelight and leave her cast to fumble their way around her, as happened in many star companies; she gave careful attention to the groupings of performers on stage and the overall visual effect. This would not have been lost on London audiences, whose attention had been consciously drawn to the staging of crowd scenes on the visit of the Meiningen Theatre in 1881, at the very time Bernhardt was breaking away from the Comédie Française.

Although Sarah's first-night performances came under constant criticism for being too long and too inept in the scene changing and for the long waits in between, this was only partially a reflection on Sarah's shortcomings, given that long waits were more customary in Paris theatres than in London venues. Mrs Alec-Tweedie, who attended the première of Sarah's *Hamlet* in Paris, brings out some of the differences between the London and Paris theatres and their conventions.[17] In particular, she cites the disruptive French convention of the *claque*, paid to applaud at particular moments in the performance using a marked text to indicate when and how many times to applaude, the comparative discomfort of the Parisian theatres, the annoying tradition of the usherettes who plague arriving spectators for tips, and the custom of the 'drop-scene' which came down at the end of each act with its advertisements for 'pills, automobiles, corsets, or tobacco'. As to the scene changing on the first night of *Hamlet*, she describes the discomfort and disruptions from the start at 8 p.m. to the finish at 2 a.m. 'Think of it ye, London first nighters!', she exclaims, 'Especially in a French theatre, where the seats are torture racks, the heat equal to Dante's Inferno, and no sweet music soothes the savage breast, only long dreary *entr' acts* and the welcome – if melancholy – three raps French playgoers know so well.'[18] Only gradually did the English convention of playing music in the *entr' acts* become an established custom. Evidently,

157

Parisian audiences were far more accustomed to delays and disruptions than their London counterparts.

Sarah always received the lion's share of performance analysis in the London reviews, but she was also responsible for introducing a number of talented French performers to London audiences. Her actresses included – to name but a few – the faithful Blanche Dufrêne, her *jeune première* for many, many years; Marie Laurent, excellent in character parts, such as Tamaryis, the gipsy-witch in *Théodora*; her sister Jeanne, whose erratic performances showed her at her best as Prince Malcolm in *Macbeth*, but hopelessly at sea as Berthe in *Le Sphinx*; Jeanne's daughter Saryta who played *ingenue* roles such as La Princesse Orlonia in *La Tosca*; and Sarah's long-standing companion, Suzanne Seylor, who frequently appeared along side the great actress in minor roles. Sarah's tendencies towards nepotism were sometimes ill-advised; this was evident particularly in her choice of leading men, when a current lover or favoured artiste ousted a more talent actor.

Among the actors who performed with Sarah, Pierre Berton, Lucien Guitry and Philippe Garnier were most favourably reviewed by London critics. Garnier made an imposing Justinien in the London *Théodora*; Berton was probably best remembered in London as the evil Scarpia in *La Tosca*; and Guitry, the caretaker manager of Sarah's Renaissance Theatre, performed consistently well as Bertrand in *La Princesse lointaine*, as Prince Hermann in *Les Rois* or as the lover, Almeiro, in *Gismonda*. Though talented in their own right, these actors never overshadowed Sarah's successes – only Coquelin, the Flambeau to her Eaglet, was equal in status, and even then it was Sarah in whom the English audiences were more interested. M. de Max, though an excellent Hormodei in *Angelo* and a thrilling and grotesque Giovanni in *Francesca da Rimini*, was generally too loud and overbearing for the English ear, as was M. Marais, Sarah's Macbeth. M. Darmont made a presentable Antony for Sarah's Cleopatra, but she over-indulged his mediocre talent in his adaptations of and performances in *Léah* and *Pauline Blanchard*.

Part of Sarah's problem with her actors was not being able to discriminate between looks and talent, and she frequently made the mistake of rewarding looks rather than acting ability, Damala and Lou Tellegen being cases in point. Others applied themselves to supporting male roles without winning great laurels, including M. Train who joined her for the first of her own London seasons to play Hippolyte et al., M. Brémont who played the unfortunate D'Aubenas in *Spiritisme* and M. Joube who replaced Tellegen as her leading man in the Coliseum seasons. A few, like Angelo, her first London Armand, were very weak performers and received bad reviews, though on the whole, for an actress who had constantly to form her own companies for her own theatres and for her tours, Sarah generally succeeded in assembling players of a high standard.

If, after all this documentation, one is forced to make a summative judgement on what impressed English audiences most about Sarah Bernhardt, then it would have to be her portraits of modern passion. Time after time, working through the different critical responses and reports of audience reactions, one receives the impression of a Victorian and Edwardian society startled into an appreciation of a performance that was blatantly sexual, physical and exotic – all the more startling because it came from a representative of the so-called 'weaker sex'. There was nothing prudish about Sarah's heroines, who were not only in love but also made love. She challenged the chaste, pure and insipid image of the English 'lady' with her heroines who knew, in the biblical sense of 'knowing', what it was to love a man. This was communicated through passionate gazes, gestures of self-abandon and seductive movements. It ran contrary to everything the Victorian ideology of the sexes stood for, and audiences loved it – and why not, if she gave them a sense of life, passion and love that bourgeois morality insisted should not exist?


What remains to be said about Sarah that can be said with any degree of certainty? That she pursued an independent life style from adolescence to old age, relying on no one to support her, whereas her energy, finance and support of others knew no bounds. She earned the money of an international star and spent it faster than she could earn it, furthering the fantastic and larger-than-life image she had decided would be the public mask to hide the private persona. She carved out her own career, made her own success and, with an impetuous and ferocious artistic temperament, never (romantic interludes aside) placed herself in a position of subservience. Her life was reflected in the romances and tragedies of her stage heroines, but one thing is absolutely clear about Sarah: unlike her heroines, she was never *helpless*. From her first visit to London in 1879 to her last in 1921, she brought pleasure and brilliance into the lives of countless spectators. She was, quite simply, 'irresistible'.

## Notes

1. For further details of the biographical drama and *Rossini* see Ernest Pronier, *Sarah Bernhardt*, p. 143.
2. Suze Rueff, *I Knew Sarah Bernhardt*, p. 228.
3. For a complete list of the roles and playlets designed for Sarah at this time, see Ernest Pronier, *Sarah Bernhardt*, pp. 347–8.
4. Maurice Rostand, *Sarah Bernhardt* (Paris: Calmann Lévy, 1950), p. 84. Lysiane and Verneuil married in 1921 but got divorced after 1923.
5. For a detailed list and documentation of Sarah's film clips, see either the annotated index by Albert Hilliard-Hughes, 'Sarah Bernhardt on the Screen', *Film Fan Monthly*, 102 (December 1969), pp. 9 and 18, or Taranow's filmography in her *Sarah Bernhardt*, pp. 271–3. Taranow's study also contains a series of stills from the 1911–12 Film d'Art version of the death scene from *La Dame aux Camélias*, with Lou Tellegen as Armand.
6. For a photograph of Sarah in *La Voyante*, see William Emboden, *Sarah Bernhardt*, p. 165.
7. Suze Rueff, *I Knew Sarah Bernhardt*, p. 234.
8. Arthur Symonds, *Eleonora Duse*, p. 27.
9. See *Pall Mall Gazette*, 16 September 1912.
10. Aside from her early short story writing, comprising *Dans les Nuages* (1878) and *A Christmas Story* published in the *Strand Magazine* (1893), Sarah's prose contributions were mostly in the form of articles for journals. In addition to *Petite Idole* in her final years, *Le Gaulois* in 1922 began serialisation of a new novel by Sarah, *Joli Sosie*, summarised by Ernest Pronier, *Sarah Bernhardt*, pp. 315–16.
11. Reynaldo Hahn, *La Grande Sarah*, p. 136.
12. The flash photography was used by Joseph Byron, and the claim to these being the first flash photographs of Sarah is made by Arthur William Row, *Sarah the Divine* (New York: Cornet Press, 1957), p. 127.

13. The series of *Izéyl* photographs can be found in A.L. Renner, *Sarah Bernhardt: Artist and Woman*, (New York: A.B. Lanck, 1896).

14. See Gerda Taranow's preface to *Sarah Bernhardt: The Art within the Legend* (Princeton: Princeton University Press, 1972), p. xiv.

15. For a summary of Sarah's teaching and pupils, see Ernest Pronier, *Sarah Bernhardt*, Appendix III, pp. 333–4.

16. Pronier discusses the influence of Sardou and Duquesnel on Sarah as *metteurs en scène* in *Sarah Bernhardt*, pp. 261–2.

17. Mrs Alec-Tweedie, *Behind the Footlights* (London: Hutchinson, 1904), pp. 158–64.

18. Ibid., pp. 160–1.

# Chronology

The following chronology relates details of Sarah Bernhardt's life and career, as well as some related theatrical events. In the interest of conciseness, the only performances to be included are a selection of those premièred in Paris and London. An asterisk * denotes an extract or one-act play.

1844    22 or 23 October, birth of Sarah-Rosine Bernhardt

1847    Birth of Ellen Terry

1860    Sarah enters the Conservatoire.

1862–3  Sarah's début at the Comédie Française.

1863–4  Her début at the Gymnase.

1864    22 December, birth of her son, Maurice.

1866    Sarah's Odéon engagement.

1869    14 January, *Le Passant*.

1870–1  Franco-Prussian War. Sarah organises a hospital at the Odéon.

1872    Sarah leaves the Odéon and re-joins the Comédie.

1874    Death of her sister Régina. 21 December, *Phèdre*.

1876    Death of Mme Sand and Sarah's mother.

1877    21 November, *Hernani*.

1878    December, partnership of Ellen Terry and Henry Irving begins at Lyceum.

1879    Sarah premières in London with the Comédie Française in *Phèdre*, *L'Etrangère*, *Le Sphinx* (Berthe), *Zaïre*, *Andromaque*, *Ruy Blas* and *Hernani*.

1880    Sarah's resignation from the Comédie. With her own company, she plays in London in *Adrienne Lecouvreur*, *Froufrou*, *Les Enfants d'Edouard*, *Jean-Marie** and *Rome vaincue**. In October, Sarah sets sail for her first tour of America.

1881    Sarah makes a grand tour of Europe. In London her programme includes the première of *La Dame aux Camélias*. The Meininger Company also visits London, and in May, Modjeska opens the season at Princess's with *Froufrou*.

1882      4 April, Sarah marries Damala. *Les Faux Ménages* and *Le Sphinx* (Blanche) are premièred in her London season. Sarah attends the celebration of the one-hundredth performance of Irving and Terry's *Romeo and Juliet*. In November, Sarah installs Maurice at the Ambigu, and on 12 December, plays *Fédora* there.

1883      Legal separation from Damala. In May, Mrs Bernard-Beere plays the lead in *Fédora* at the Haymarket. Later, Sarah plays in *Fédora* for the first time in London. In September, Sarah begins management at the Porte Saint-Martin until 1886. 17 September, Sarah plays *Froufrou* in Paris.

1884      Sarah's Paris productions include *Macbeth* (21 May), which she later premières in London, and *Théodora* (26 December).

1885      Sarah premières *Théodora* in London, while Hading and Damala appear in *Le Maître de Forges*. 30 December, she plays *Marion Delorme* in Paris.

1886      Spring, Sarah leaves for a tour of North and South America. Death of Jarrett; Maurice Grau becomes Sarah's secretary.

1887      Summer, she returns to Paris, where she moves to Boulevard Pereire, the residence she will keep for the rest of her life. 24 November, she plays *La Tosca* in Paris. 29 December, Maurice marries Terka Jablonowska.

1888      April, begins twelve-month European tour, during which she premières *La Tosca* and *Francillon* in London. December, Ellen Terry's Lady Macbeth.

1889      18 April, Sarah plays *Léna*, which she later premières in London. Death of Damala.

1890      3 January, Sarah plays *Jeanne d'Arc* in Paris and later premières it in London. 23 October, she plays *Cléopâtre* in Paris.

1891      January, sets out on a world tour, which lasts until 1893.

1892      In London, Sarah premières *Cléopâtre*, *Pauline Blanchard* and *Léah*.

1893      November, Sarah takes over the Renaissance until January

1899; on 6 November, she plays *Les Rois* there. In London, Mrs Bernard-Beere plays in *A Woman of No Importance* in April; Mrs Patrick Campbell plays in *The Second Mrs Tanqueray* in May; Duse makes her London début in *La Dame aux Camélias*, and Bartet appears at Drury Lane.

1894  24 January, Sarah plays *Izéyl* in Paris and later premières it in London along with *Les Rois* and *La Femme de Claude*. In June, Réjane conquers London in *Mme Sans Gêne*. 31 October, Sarah plays *Gismonda* in Paris.

1895  5 April, Sarah plays *La Princesse lointaine* in Paris and later prémieres it in London, along with *Gismonda* and *Magda*, rivalling Duse in the latter play. Also in London, Mrs Pat plays *Fedora*.

1896  Brief American tour. Her summer season in London contains no new roles. 3 December, Sarah plays in *Lorenzaccio* in Paris, and on 9 December, Henry Bauer organises a *Journée Sarah Bernhardt*.

1897  3 February, *Spiritisme* opens in Paris and on 14 April, *La Samaritaine*. In June, Sarah opens the Renaissance to Duse. Maurice and Sarah quarrel over the Dreyfus affair; Sarah supports Zola's campaign, but Maurice is anti. *Lorenzaccio* and *Spiritisme* are premièred in London. Also in London, Réjane appears as Froufrou at the Lyric.

1898  Sarah prémieres *Lysiane* and *Julie* in London. 28 October, she opens *Médée* in Paris.

1899  January, Sarah takes over the Nations until her death; renamed the Théâtre Sarah Bernhardt. The theatre is refurbished, and on 20 May, *Hamlet* opens. *Hamlet* later premières in London.

1900  15 March, Sarah opens *L'Aiglon* in Paris. London receives a summer visit from a Japanese company, with Sada Yocco. November, Sarah embarks on an American tour with Coquelin until May 1901.

1901  Sarah premières *L'Aiglon* and *Cyrano de Bergerac* in London, and in June, Réjane plays Sapho. Death of Queen Victoria; Edward VII ascends throne.

1902  May, begins European tour, including her first performances in Germany. Sarah premières *Francesca da Rimini* in London. In

July, Irving and Terry close at the Lyceum. 23 December, she opens *Théroigne de Méricourt* in Paris.

1903    7 February, Sarah opens as Hermione in *Andromaque* in Paris and on 6 March opens *Werther*. In London, she premières *Andromaque, Bohèmos\*, Sapho* and *Plus que reine*. 15 December, she opens *La Sorcière* in Paris.

1904    Sarah premières *La Sorcière* and *Pelléas et Mélisande* in London. The Barker-Vedrenne management begins at the Court, promoting the new writing of Shaw, Galsworthy, etc. In December, Stoll's Coliseum opens.

1905    7 February, Sarah opens *Angelo* in Paris and on 8 April *Esther* (*travesti*). In London, Sarah's version of *Adrienne Lecouvreur* premières along with *Angelo*. August, American tour.

1906    Tour ends in June.

1907    Sarah prémieres *Le Réveil* in London. End of Barker-Vedrenne management at the Court. 25 December, Sarah makes a *travesti* appearance in *La Belle au bois dormant* in Paris.

1908    Death of Sardou. September, Sarah begins her last grand tour of Europe, which ends in February 1909. Miss Horniman purchases the Gaiety Theatre, Manchester, for her company, heralding new writing and performing.

1909    25 November, Sarah opens *Le Procès de Jeanne d'Arc* in Paris. Death of Coquelin

1910    September–October, Sarah's first Coliseum visit. October, she begins an American tour.

1911    Sarah is at the Coliseum again during September and October and premières *Le Procès de Jeanne d'Arc\**. In October, Réjane performs at the Hippodrome. 23 November, Sarah opens *Lucrèce Borgia* in Paris.

1912    11 April, Sarah opens *Elisabeth, Reine d'Angleterre* in Paris. At the Coliseum again in September and October, she premières *Lucrèce Borgia\*, Elisabeth, Reine d'Angleterre\** and *Une Nuit de Noël sous La Terreur\**. 23 October, London pays tribute to Sarah's 69th birthday. November, she begins another American tour until December 1913.

1913    During her September–October season at the Coliseum, Sarah prémieres *La Samaritaine\**, and *La Mort de Cléopâtre\**. 11 October,

165

King and Queen attend Charity Night. December, Sarah decorated with Legion of Honour.

1914   Outbreak of War. Stage dominated by light entertainment and patriotic pieces throughout the war years.

1915   February, amputation of Sarah's leg. 6 November, she plays in *Les Cathédrales\** in Paris.

1916.  In January, Sarah brings to the Coliseum *Les Cathédrales\**, *Du Théâtre au Champ d'Honnêté\** and in April *Une d'elles\**. Vesta Tilley rallies the troops with her military numbers. Farewell tour of America, which ends in 1918.

1918   Death of Rostand shortly after Armistice.

1920   1 April, Sarah opens *Athalie* in Paris and on 6 November, *Daniel*.

1921   Sarah brings *Daniel* to London, for her last season on the London stage. 18 October, she opens *La Gloire* in Paris.

1922   13 April, Sarah opens *La Mort de Molière* in Paris and on 20 April *Régine Armand*.

1923   26 March, death of Sarah Bernhardt, leaving filming of *La Voyante* unfinished. Requiem mass for Sarah in Westminster Cathedral, attended by a vast crowd, including Ellen Terry.

# Select Bibliography

## Works by Sarah Bernhardt

Bernhardt, Sarah, *Dans les Nuages, Impressions d'une chaise* (Paris: Charpentier, 1878), trans. *In the Clouds*, contained in *The Memoirs of Sarah Bernhardt* (New York & London: Peebles Press, 1977)

——, *L'Aveu* (Paris: Ollendorff, 1888)

——, *A Christmas Story*, trans. in *The Strand Magazine*, December 1893, pp. 711–14

——, 'Men's Roles as Played by Women', *Harper's Bazaar*, 33 (15 December 1900), pp. 2113–15

——, (1907) *Ma Double vie: mémoires de Sarah Bernhardt*, 2 vols (Paris: Charpentier, 1923), trans. as *My Double Life. Memoirs of Sarah Bernhardt* (London: Heinemann, 1907) and (London: Bles, 1924)

——, (1907) *Adrienne Lecouvreur* (Paris: Charpentier & Fasquelle, 1908)

——, *Un Coeur d'homme* (Paris: Charpentier & Fasquelle, 1911)

——, *Petite idole* (Paris: Nilsson, 1920), trans. as *The Idol of Paris* (London: Cecil Palmer, 1921)

——, *L'Art du théâtre* (Paris: Nilsson, 1923), trans. by H.J. Stenning as *The Art of the Theatre* (London: Bles, 1924)

## Biographies

Agate, May, *Madame Sarah* (London: Home & Van Thal, 1945)

Baring, Maurice, *Sarah Bernhardt* (London: Nelson, 1938)

Bernhardt, Lysiane, *Sarah Bernhardt. ma grand' mère* (Paris. Editions du Pavois, 1945)

Berton, Thérèse, *Sarah Bernhardt as I Knew Her: Memoirs of Mme Pierre Berton as told to Basil Woon* (London: Hurst & Blackett, 1923)

Castelot, André, *Sarah Bernhardt* (Paris: Le Livre Contemporain, 1961)

Colombier, Marie, *Les Mémoires de Sarah Barnum* (Paris, 1884), trans. as *The Life and Memoirs of Sarah Barnum*, ed. H.L. Williams (London: Crown, 1884)

Emboden, William, *Sarah Bernhardt* (London: Studio Vista/ Macmillan, 1974)

Geller, G.-J., *Sarah Bernhardt* (Paris: Gallimard, 1931)

Hahn, Reynaldo, *La Grande Sarah* (Paris: Hachette, 1929)

Huret, Jules, *Sarah Bernhardt: acteurs et actrices d'aujourd'hui* (Paris: Juven, 1899)

Pronier, Ernest, *Sarah Bernhardt: une vie au théâtre* (Geneva: Alex. Jullien, n.d.)

Renner, A.L., *Sarah Bernhardt: Artist and Woman* (New York: Blanck, 1896)

Richardson, Joanna, *Sarah Bernhardt* (London: Max Reinhardt, 1959)

———, *Sarah Bernhardt and her World* (London: Weidenfeld & Nicolson, 1977)

Rostand, Maurice, *Sarah Bernhardt* (Paris: Calmann Lévy, 1950)

Row, Arthur William, *Sarah the Divine* (New York: Cornet Press, 1957)

Rueff, Suze, *I Knew Sarah Bernhardt* (London: Muller, 1951)

Salmon, Eric, *Bernhardt and the Theatre of her Time* (Westport, Conn. & London: Greenwood Press, 1984)

Taranow, Gerda, *Sarah Bernhardt: The Art within the Legend* (Princeton: Princeton University Press, 1972)

Verneuil, Louis, *La Vie merveilleuse de Sarah Bernhardt* (Montréal: Editions Variétés, 1942), trans. by Ernest Boyd as *The Fabulous Life of Sarah Bernhardt* (New York & London: Harper, 1942)

## Works with Chapters on Sarah Bernhardt

Alec-Tweedie, Mrs., *Behind the Footlights* (London: Hutchinson, 1904)

Knepler, Henry, *The Gilded Stage* (London: Constable, 1968)

Scott, Clement (1900), *Some Notable Hamlets* (New York & London: Benjamin Blom, 1969)

Stokes, John, Michael R. Booth and Susan Bassnett, *Bernhardt Terry Duse: The Actress in her Time* (Cambridge: Cambridge

University Press 1988)
Symons, Arthur (1927), *Eleonora Duse* (New York & London: Benjamin Blom, 1969)

## Newspaper Sources

*Daily News*
*Daily Telegraph*
*Era*
*Morning Post*
*Pall Mall Gazette*
*Speaker*
*Spectator*
*Star*
*Theatre*
*The Times*
*Westminster Gazette*

## Special Collections

Marandet Collection: Nineteenth Century French Drama, 1830–1900 (University of Warwick Library)

# Index